CREAT
WEAL
ON T
WEB

with QUIXTAR

The Phenomenal New Business Opportunity that Makes E-commerce Work for You

Cynthia Stewart-Copier
with Jennifer Basye Sander

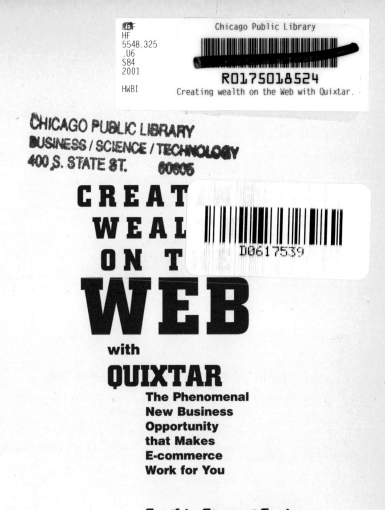

Adams Media Corporation
Holbrook, Massachusetts

Dedication

To Don and Ruth Storms and Leo and Amy Grant for blazing the trail to success and for always being willing to give their love, support, and help to all of us who are creating wealth with Quixtar.

Published by
Adams Media Corporation
260 Center Street, Holbrook, MA 02343
www.adamsmedia.com

ISBN: 1-58062-473-1

Printed in Canada.

J I H G F E D C B A

Library of Congress Cataloging-in-Publication Data
Stewart-Copier, Cynthia.
Creating wealth on the Web with Quixtar / by Cynthia Stewart-Copier with Jennifer Basye Sander.
p. cm.
ISBN 1-58062-473-1
1. Quixtar.com. 2. Electronic commerce--United States. 3. Internet marketing--United States. I. Sander, Jennifer Basye, 1958- II. Title.
HF5548.325.U6 S84 2001
658.8'4--dc21 00-050251

This publication is designed to provide accurate and authoritative information with regard to the subject matter covered. It is sold with the understanding that the publisher is not engaged in rendering legal, accounting, or other professional advice. If legal advice or other expert assistance is required, the services of a competent professional person should be sought.

—From a *Declaration of Principles* jointly adopted by a Committee of the American Bar Association and a Committee of Publishers and Associations

Launching any business venture, including the ventures described in this book, is likely to raise a variety of legal and financial issues. It may be advisable to obtain professional legal and financial advice in connection with such issues. The ideas and suggestions contained in this book are not intended to replace the advice of legal or financial professionals. The content of this book, including its title and subtitle, reflect the views of its authors and not necessarily those of Adams Media Corporation.

QUIXTAR is a service mark of Quixtar Investments, Inc. This book is not sponsored by Quixtar Investments, Inc.

This book is available at quantity discounts for bulk purchases.
For information, call 1-800-872-5627.

Contents

Acknowledgments

As time goes by, the number of people to whom I find myself indebted seems to grow exponentially and I find myself struggling to find a way to say "thank you" when there are so many people who have been such powerful influences in my life, as well as in this project. The names that follow can only be a representative sampling. To those named and unnamed, I extend my heartfelt gratitude for your contribution to making *Creating Wealth on the Web with Quixtar* a success.

First and foremost, I thank my family. Without them I would be lost. To my children, Tyler and Rebecca, for giving me a huge reason to dream big, and a special thanks to my daughter, Rachel, for holding us all together through the past few months.

Jennifer Basye Sander for encouraging me to stretch beyond my comfort zone. Sheree Bykofsky, my agent, for her continual support and belief in my dream. Adams Media Corporation, especially Jere Calmes, my editor, and Dawn Thompson for their vision and determination to help this book become a success.

A special thanks to each of the IBOs who generously and graciously gave their time to share their stories and secrets of success. And to all of the Diamonds who have built their own network marketing business, created wealth, and dared to dream big!

Foreword

In many ways, network marketing seems perfectly designed for the Information Age. It enables people to work from home, to manage their own time, and to earn a residual income commensurate with their efforts.

Increasingly, entrepreneurs are doing their marketing online. Network marketers today use voice mail broadcasts, fax-on-demand services, e-mail auto-responders, and interactive Web sites not simply as adjuncts to their businesses but as the basis for them. They live, move, and prosper in a high-tech environment that many corporate executives only theorize about.

Creating Wealth on the Web with Quixtar by Cynthia Stewart-Copier with Jennifer Basye Sander tells about one company, Quixtar, that has moved decisively into the Web-based network-marketing environment of the future.

I wrote about Quixtar in my 1999 book *Wave 4*, noting that companies such as this—which combine the mass-marketing clout of the Internet with the personal touch of real, live human sales agents—could prove to be a "magic bullet" that will help make e-commerce more user-friendly.

The authors have done an excellent job of presenting both the opportunities and challenges of conducting business in a "Wave 4" company. Their book offers a wealth of practical pointers useful to any cyber-preneur, regardless of company affiliation. Cynthia's hands-on experience as a network marketer and author, combined with Jennifer's formidable skills as a writer, editor, storyteller, and business visionary, have created a wonderful read—together, they make an impressive team.

I highly recommend this book, both as an introduction to an important new company, and as a manual for e-commerce success.

Richard Poe
author of *Wave 4: Networking Marketing in the 21st Century*

Introduction

When Cynthia asked me to write the introduction for *Creating Wealth on the Web with Quixtar*, I was skeptical at first. Was this yet another person attempting to take advantage of my position in the industry or, worse yet, of the great leaders in my extensive downline? Yet, after spending several hours with Cynthia I realized that not only did she have the right intentions, but she also has a keen sense of this business and the ability to articulate a message that I feel will help others. And so, I am happy to tell you that this book is one that I believe will help both current IBOs continue to build and develop their own businesses, as well as assist those who are looking, perhaps for the first time, at e-commerce. It offers an accurate account of the industry and, in particular, the inner workings of Quixtar and the opportunity it offers anyone with a dream and the determination to make that dream a reality.

That being said, I must tell you that I am biased in my opinions of this business and of Quixtar. You would expect me to be, wouldn't you? My business spans the globe, and last year alone I earned more than $5 million in compensation plan money. For newcomers, that means the total of my bonuses paid by this corporation. My income in my other corporations exceeded even that figure, but it is important to add that all my corporations started from the money I earned from this business. So, am I a little biased, you ask? You bet I am! Wouldn't you be?

Before this business came along, I was a young, broke kid, living in an alley in Rome, New York. And my future? It was dismal at best. So, although I may be biased, it comes from the results I've seen and the rewards I now enjoy from this business. This is the best business on planet earth—period! There is nothing else that even comes close. We have the history, the incredible numbers of people, and the billions of dollars of volume to prove it, and it just keeps getting better and better.

So sit back, relax, and read through the pages of this book. Here, you will unlock some secrets of success with Quixtar. You will learn some tips that I have taught for years and that have helped me foster many millionaires in my own business. Follow these simple steps and you will be on a path toward building your own dreams. Anything is possible for those who dare to dream big!

Dexter Yager
October 2000

Preface

The Age of Aquarius melted quietly away with the passing of the last century, and the Age of Entrepreneurs is upon us! Doesn't it sometimes seem like everyone you know is starting up a business? Making plans, saving up their money, moving to a hot new area where office space is still cheap . . . starting your own business is a major topic of conversation everywhere you turn.

But are we *all* cut out to be "dotcom" CEOs? Or to buy an expensive bagel franchise? Is there a rewarding business that we can build together with our spouses, our friends, or with our children, one that doesn't require millions of dollars, hundreds of hours of work per week, or countless airplane trips? Yes, there is. And you hold the beginnings of it in your hands; this very book can help you achieve success in that business.

Last year I spent many months working on a network-marketing handbook for women called *Dream Big!* I interviewed hundreds of successful women who had built up their families' incomes with network-marketing businesses. And I was often asked, "Cynthia, which company are you with?" I was reluctant to answer the question because I didn't want *Dream Big!* to focus too heavily on any one company but rather on the fantastic opportunities that were there available. I hemmed and hawed and tried to sidestep the question as best I could. I developed a Web site (*www.dreambig.com*) to help other entrepreneurs reach the level of success they dream of achieving.

I have been in network-marketing for two decades now, and I am more excited by the industry now than ever before. I have been so pleased by my own incredible business success in the past year that I think the time is right for me to identify myself with one company. That company is . . . Quixtar!

Have you heard of Quixtar yet? Chances are you've picked up *Creating Wealth on the Web with Quixtar* because you've heard the name, you've read a bit about it, or you've just started to learn how to build income with Quixtar. You are curious—what is all the fuss about this new Internet company? Well, you have reached for the right part of the bookstore shelf, because with *Creating Wealth on the Web with Quixtar* I will tell you all you need to know about Quixtar to decide if this is the right business for you. And if it is, I'll take you by the hand and try to give you the expert's perspective on how to build your business from the ground up to the stars!

I feel compelled to write this book to share with you the excitement that is swirling around this exciting e-commerce company. Founded by major industry names, Quixtar is making it possible for ordinary folks—not just "dotcom geeks"—to get involved in harnessing the awesome power of the Internet to build a business that has the potential to generate a handsome income and a rewarding work life.

So, join with me now in beginning your exploration of the world of Quixtar. It could change your life. . . .

The first section of the book, Part One, is called **Dream It!** In these chapters I will help you shape your desire for financial security and a business of your own. Together, you and I will explore the idea of a dream business, how your own thoughts have a huge impact on your success, why you should start your own business, and what the heck is going on when people talk about e-commerce. And then, I'll introduce you to Quixtar.

In the second part, Part Two, **Dare It!,** I will help you get a sense of what it takes to succeed in this business, and how you can follow the methods used by many of the industry leaders.

And then once you have absorbed this exciting information, I will ask you to **Do It!** in Part Three. You will learn the role that personal motivation plays in business success, and what a tremendously powerful effect your own personal motivation can have on those who join the business with you. You'll also read about folks just like you who, after learning the facts, have decided to build their own Quixtar-affiliated businesses.

So what are we waiting for? Let's start learning about Quixtar!

—*Cynthia Stewart-Copier*
February 2001

Sign up today for Cynthia's weekly motivational newsletter at www.DareToDreamBig.com.

PART ONE

Dream It!

CHAPTER ONE

Build Your Dream Business

WOW, WHAT A NAME FOR AN OPENING CHAPTER—*build your dream business*. Is that a lofty goal, or what? With this book, I plan to help you do just that—help you build a business of your own that will take you down the road to your dreams.

But before we learn about dream businesses—what they are and how to build them—I'd like to let you know a little something about me. I'd like to share a story about my early days in business. The more you know about me, the better you will understand what compelled me to write the book you now hold in your hands, the very book that I hope will allow you to follow your dreams. . . .

A Little Personal History

It was 1986. I was 30 years old and had just closed the books on my most profitable year in the recreational vehicle business. Our gross sales were up almost 30 percent from the previous year. I was riding high, that is, until I finished reading the annual report and my eye caught the bottom line—we were in the red almost a quarter of a million dollars! How can that be possible, I wondered? With sales in the millions, up more than $2 million from the previous year, why didn't we make any money?

The Nightmare Begins

It all started the day my husband began his quest for a dream business. I was skeptical the day he told me of his new dream, to purchase an existing lot for our recreational vehicle business, right on the Interstate in Northern California. We were already struggling just to meet the lease payments on our present location, and with interest rates on the rise, our flooring costs were up as well. But he was convinced—absolutely certain, in fact—that moving from our present location, which was five miles out of town, to this new location, right in the middle of the city on the Interstate, would be our ticket to success. And he was right. Although our overhead was more than tripled by that move, our sales began to skyrocket in that first year. We were elated.

We ran some splashy ads and started a marathon of television and radio advertising. There was hardly a spot for customers to park in our three acres of paved, freeway-frontage property as we had increased our inventory to capacity. We installed a gigantic flagpole, complete with an impressive American flag, which blew side by side with our new and enormous sign, directing traffic to our newest enterprise. And then we waited. We waited for the customers and the money to come pouring in. And they did—for the first few months.

It didn't take long for reality to set in, however. Each month we had to ring up $250,000 in sales just to keep the doors open. Our overhead was staggering, and costs were mounting. Every time we turned around, it seemed that some creditor had his or her hand out. Almost everyday started with my accountant standing there in front of me, holding a pen and the company checkbook in hand.

"Sign here," he'd say. I signed there. And I signed . . . and signed . . . and signed. Meanwhile, our flooring costs (the interest and overhead charges on inventory) were rising with the interest rates. I began to sweat the monthly flooring checks, worried that I had not gotten my latest check out in time to beat the bank. Our inventory had to be constantly updated—new colors, new floor plans, even new manufacturing lines were added. Old inventory had to go on clearance and new employees were hired. And our sales staff was forever asking, "Can you give me an advance against my next week's commission?" I'd sign another check.

My husband and I were both working, often 140 cumulative hours a week, coming home exhausted and worried about meeting the next week's bills. Our dream business was turning into a nightmare. Then, as if that weren't enough, my husband went in for a simple outpatient surgery and landed in the hospital for over two months! That began the fight for his life, and he struggled with multiple surgeries and serious health issues for the next two years. Meanwhile, the bills kept coming in. It seemed like everyone got the money, except me.

Valuable Lessons Cost Money

They say that experience is the best teacher. If this is true, then I have a Ph.D. in selling RVs. I spent more than 14 years in the recreational vehicle business and, in the end, had less money than when I began. Yes, I learned some truly valuable lessons, and it cost me big money to learn them. Starting our dream business was the second best decision I made in the 1980s. The very best decision was to close my business, sell the land, and end the nightmare.

I learned that dreaming about opening a business doesn't make it a dream business. In other words, not all businesses are created equal. Some are better than others, and that's the truth!

Not all businesses are created equal—
some really are better than others!

What Is a Dream Business?

So how would you describe your dream business? Would it be an established franchise like McDonald's or Starbucks? Would it be a retail clothing store or a bakery? I took the liberty of making some comparisons that you may find interesting and certainly financially important as you contemplate your dream business. The following is a list of characteristics of a dream business versus a traditional business. Perhaps, when you compare them side by side, as I did, it will be easy for you to see that owning a dream business would be much more attractive than owning a traditional business—and more profitable too!

Dream Business	vs.	Traditional Business
Low start-up costs		Every penny you have, plus more that you borrow
Low overhead costs		Monthly lease on building, land, equipment, etc.
Little or no inventory		Huge expense of inventory
No employees		Employees
Set your own hours		Often work seven days a week
Recession-proof		Success dependent on seasons, economy, or trends

DREAM BUSINESS	VS.	TRADITIONAL BUSINESS *(continued)*
No territory restrictions		Limited territory
No advertising		Expensive advertising costs
Unlimited income		Income limited
Experienced mentors or advisors		You are your own mentor/advisor
Residual income		Trade time for money
No licenses, employee payroll, state tax reports, or burdening bookkeeping		Heavy bookkeeping required

So, what do you think? You can see that there is a big difference between a dream business and the realities of a traditional business. Perhaps you are thinking that the dream business sounds too good to be true. That is what I thought at first, and then I found out some interesting information that changed the paradigm I held in my mind. As you look over the list, you might be thinking, "Hey, if there really were a business that had all of the advantages of a dream business and none of the disadvantages of a traditional business, I'd be foolish not to give it a serious look."

I agree. As you'll soon discover, there is such a dream business. It has all of the benefits previously listed, plus several more that we'll discuss in future chapters. For now, just remember that if you can find a business that meets the following six criteria, you have found yourself a true dream business:

1. Low investment and overhead (home-based or cottage business is perfect)
2. Residual income (do the work once and receive payment year after year)
3. Global market potential (opportunity conduct business internationally)

4. Possibility of being inherited or sold (generational income, can be bequeathed to children)
5. Diversified product line (large product availability as opposed to one line, such as nutritional items or cosmetics)
6. Duplicable characteristics (cookie-cutter system that can be taught and repeated over and over)

When you find a business that offers all of these six criteria, you've got a sure winner. But remember, if even one of the criteria is missing, you lessen your percentages for success and end up with just another traditional business in disguise. It is just like dialing a phone number or sending an e-mail—if you miss only one number, you can't get through.

To build a dream business, first find a business that meets the criteria of a dream business.

Money Isn't Everything

Money isn't everything, but in the end, it is the only thing that makes a business truly successful. In the end, if the bottom line is in the red, no matter how much you may love what you do, you'll have a difficult time finding a way to continue doing it.

Some people tell me that money isn't what people are really motivated by—what they are really searching for—it's the *benefits* that money can bring or what money can buy that they are really after. So, maybe owning your own dream business isn't what you really started out to find, but you found out that some of the *benefits* of a dream business were what you really wanted. Let's take another look at the dream business criteria and discuss the *benefits* of owning your own.

Number One: Low Investment and Overhead

Start a Dream Business . . . and Forget About:

- Raising big sums of capital
- Renting a huge store or office building
- Trying to collect unpaid invoices
- Paying for advertising
- Worrying about a shrinking market

According to the Small Business Administration, the number one reason that businesses fail is that they are undercapitalized. When your expensive overhead is greater than your sales, you just get further and further behind. I know this is true from personal experience. Even if sales were down at my dealership, I still had to pay the bills.

A dream business would have a low start-up cost, under $200 would be ideal, and low monthly maintenance. That would mean no employees, no big lease payments, no huge inventory requirements—no *anything* that rang up big fixed monthly expenses.

It's because of these benefits that more and more people are turning to running home-based businesses. It is just plain common sense. A one-minute commute from the bedroom to your office and your overhead is zero! A high-powered, high-tech office can be in your spare bedroom, or what about that formal dining room that you only use twice a year? You can open your office, complete with computer, Internet service, fax, scanner, business phone, cell phone, and copy machine for less than what it costs me to take my family to Disney World for a weekend.

Number Two: Residual Income

Getting paid over and over again after having done the work only one time is my idea of a dream business. How about you? A classic example is the stock market. Just this afternoon I sat with my friend, Jennifer, and checked out her online stock investments. Let's say it takes you 100 hours of work at your job to earn $1,000. To earn $100,000, using the time-for-dollars exchange formula, you'd have to work 10,000 hours at $10 per hour, which would come out to working 40 hours a week for almost five years.

More Than Money

Money isn't what people are really motivated by—what they are really searching for—it's the *benefits* that money can bring or what money can buy that they are really after.

Contrast this scenario to investing that $1,000 one time in a high-return stock. It would continue to earn money for you year after year. For example, if you had purchased $1,000 worth of America Online stock less than five years ago, how much do you think it would be worth today? $10,000, maybe? $100,000? Give up? Try more than $500,000! That's right—over a half million dollars on a $1,000 investment—and in less than five years.

This enormous return on investment is the result of a concept called compounding, or exponential growth, which we'll discuss later. Compounding and residual income are both examples of what happens when you escape the time-for-money trap—you do the work once, and it keeps paying you over and over again!

Make plans now to escape the time-for-money trap and get paid over and over again for work you did long ago!

Number Three: Global Market Potential

The world is literally at our fingertips today, and it has never been truer than with the Internet. We can take an order from Italy on Friday and have it in the customer's hands by the following Wednesday. So why settle for a niche market or a postage-stamp territory when the whole world can be yours? This global market is not a new concept. Big businesses have understood this principle for years. Did you know that 60 percent of Coca-Cola Company's business is overseas? McDonald's, Wendy's, and Taco Bell are expanding faster internationally than they are in the United States. With such a tremendous world market, why limit our efforts to a tiny slice of the pie?

Number Four: Possibility of Being Inherited and Sold

Making the decision to start your dream business is certainly the first step toward living your dreams. The second step is to plan your life five, 10, or 20 years from now—your exit strategy. You may want to cash in early.

I certainly would sleep better if I knew my family and loved ones would be taken care of if something happened to me. Wouldn't you? Wouldn't you feel great if you were building equity and generating income? When my husband was hospitalized, our income took a nosedive. Wouldn't yours? And when we were looking to cash out, it wasn't even an option for our kids. A job will never be sellable, inheritable, or willable. A dream business is both!

Ask yourself, "Is your income inheritable? What would happen to your family if you died suddenly?"

Number Five: Diversified Product Line

If you could offer a customer, or potential business partner for that matter, everything from cars to caviar, or peanut butter to pâté, wouldn't it make sense that you would sell more product? Supply and demand, right? If you can offer a wide variety of products across several different markets, especially if those items include consumables—toilet paper, office supplies, vitamins, coffee, and cosmetics—you would need fewer customers. If I wanted to generate $7,500 in gross monthly sales, I could sell $100 of product to 75 people. However, if I could offer those same 75 people more products that replaced what they were already buying each month, say $300 worth, I would have increased my sales to $22,500 almost effortlessly.

Same number of people, less work, more volume. That means more profit for you! A dream business has a diversified product line, one that ideally includes consumable goods.

Number Six: Duplicable

Ever heard the statement, "Birds of a feather flock together?" If you want to hit it big in business, be a real success, wouldn't it make sense to do what the successful people have already done? Duplication isn't new. It is just common sense. Take, for example, McDonald's—what is the secret of their success? Do you really think it is their hamburgers? When Ray Kroc started McDonald's and later franchised these stores, he learned the power of duplication—teaching a simple, proven system of success to others. And it worked!

Like franchising, independent business owners (IBOs) follow the training system of their successful leaders. Then they in turn teach those same training system steps to their new IBOs, duplicating the pattern for success. Those newest IBOs teach their new people, who teach their new people, and so on. This is how successful businesses have been built for decades. This cookie-cutter training method is often known as a turnkey system. It simplifies or automates part of the business, making it easier for ordinary people to operate them.

A strong business model will be one in which training material is easy to attain. Books, tapes, video conferencing, and meetings or seminars are a must for any serious moneymaker. A dream business must have a proven system of success—one that is simple to understand and easy to teach to others.

Definition Please!

IBO stands for independent business owner. What is an independent business owner, you ask? It simply means an individual who owns his or her *own* business and who has registered with Quixtar to do business with its Web site.

As an IBO, you have the opportunity to earn cash bonuses based on volume created by driving traffic (shoppers) to Quixtar.

Speed Up the Process

Now that you understand the six criteria for creating a dream business, would you like to learn how to speed up your success and see the money roll in even faster than you might imagine? Sure you would! I have known people who have made tons of money and built incredible dream businesses from their kitchen tables with an ordinary phone and piece of paper and nothing else! But why run with the dinosaurs when you can fly with the rockets? Just because "that's the way it's always been done" doesn't make it the best way to do business in the new millennium.

There is a better way—the Internet! The Internet changes everything about business, making it bigger and faster if you know how to use it to your advantage. Every dream business will include an Internet-based component to it. We'll be discussing this in detail in Part Two: Dare It!, but for now, let's get a running jump toward success! In Chapter Two we will be talking about money—making a lot of it that is! Think big and cash in big.

CHAPTER TWO

Think Big to Win Big

What does it mean to win big, you might ask? Winning big can mean many wonderful things. Winning big might mean prosperity: beautiful homes, luxury cars, financial security, travel, providing opportunities for your children. Winning big might mean having the respect of those you admire. It might mean having leadership among or admiration from the people in your business or social world. Winning big might mean freedom: freedom from financial worries or failure. It might mean freedom to make choices for yourself and your family, such as where you live, what schools your children attend, where you spend your vacations and for what length of time. Winning big might mean achieving a positive self-image, continually growing personally and spiritually, and developing lasting friendships. Winning big means something different for everyone. But one thing everyone does agree on: winning big means success!

What Is the Secret?

Why is one person sad and another happy? Why is one person prosperous and another poor? Why is one person fearful and anxious and another full of confidence and faith? Why does one person have a luxurious home while another lives out a meager existence? Why is one person a success and another person a failure? What is the difference, the secret? Is there an answer to these questions in the workings of your mind? There certainly is!

What Do You Get When You Win BIG?

BIG HOUSE
BIG INCOME
BIG CAR
BIG SUCCESS!
BIG SATISFACTION!

Mind is the master-power that moulds and makes,
And man is mind, and evermore he takes
The tool of thought, and, shaping what he wills,
Brings for a thousand joys, a thousand ills: -
He thinks in secret, and it comes to pass;
Environment is but his looking glass.
—*James Allen,* As a Man Thinketh

Thoughts Are Things

I have read many inspirational books in my life, and I'd like to share some of the most meaningful passages I've discovered along the way—passages that have truly made a difference in the way I look at life, the way I live my life, and what I now believe is possible. And I'm confident that these ideas will have a profound effect on your thinking, too.

In his book, *As a Man Thinketh*, author James Allen says that the truth of life is that we are the makers of ourselves. By the virtue of our thoughts, which we choose and encourage, our mind is the master weaver, both of our inner garment of character and outer garment of circumstance. He says, "The aphorism, 'As a man thinketh in his heart so is he,' not only embraces the whole of a man's being but it is so comprehensive as to reach out to every condition and circumstance of his life. A man is literally what he thinks, his character being the complete sum of all his thoughts."

James Allen uses an example of a plant: that as a plant grows from, and could not be without, a seed, so does every act of man spring from the hidden seed of our thoughts. There has never been an act we have performed that was not proceeded by a thought.

Henry Van Dyke says it this way:
I hold it true that thoughts are things;
They're endowed with bodies and breath and wings:
And that we send them forth to fill,
The world with good results, or ill.
That which we call our secret thought
Speeds forth to earth's remotest spot,
Leaving its blessings or its woes
Like tracks behind it as it goes.

We build our future, thought by thought,
For good or ill, yet know it not.
Yet so the universe was wrought.
Thought is another name for fate;
Choose then thy destiny and wait,
For love brings love and hate brings hate.

Author Earl Nightingale once wrote, "We are what we think about." Thoughts are things. Every word we have spoken, every step we have taken, every action we have made first began with a thought, whether conscious or not.

The minute you start making your thoughts work *for* you, instead of *against* you, is the exact moment your life will change dramatically.

Let's look at what can happen when we just drift through life without consciously questioning our thoughts. . . .

Automatic Pilot

When I was a young girl, the hot days of summer often found my family at the lake. Boating was my all-time favorite summer activity. The sound of the motor combined with the wind in my face seemed to offer great relief from the scorching heat of the Texas sun. We would jump into the boat, waves slapping against the sides, until we found the perfect spot for swimming. My father, not at all interested in swimming, would be looking for the perfect spot for fishing. Determining that he had found just the right place to catch the "big one," he would lull the motor to a crawl and set the automatic pilot to maintain a very slow course.

Before he could even get in his first cast, my brothers and I would splash into the icy cold water of that deep lake and promise to swim away from his perfect fishing place. I was a strong swimmer and would swim quite a distance from the boat. After getting a sufficiently far distance between me and my two younger brothers, I would float on my back, the sun baking my face, looking up at the blue sky and puffy white clouds while my younger brothers would take turns dunking each other with squeals of delight. Soon, my father would whistle and we would each return to the boat while he looked once more for the perfect spot to catch the big one. Determining once again to have found it, he would again lull the motor and make us promise to swim quietly away from his fishing place.

On one occasion he forgot to reset the automatic pilot in the boat and I wasn't watching close enough. When I finally looked up he seemed to have drifted quite away from us. Both of my brothers and I began to call out, "Hey, Daddy, over here." When he turned the front of the boat and crept carefully toward us, we asked him where he was going. He explained the automatic pilot, how it worked, and what had happened when he forgot to reset it. It had taken him, unknowingly, back on the previous course he had programmed in, which was not the course he had wanted.

Change the Program!

Later in life I realized that each of us has an automatic pilot of sorts—a program in our minds. Teachers, parents, siblings, family, and peers have helped us set some of these programs. Other thoughts we have created ourselves, and whether or not they are "true," we operate our own course in life based upon the settings. Often, in order to change the course of our lives, we need to reprogram our thinking about not only our own selves but also about what we think we are capable of, or think we deserve. If it is true that we get what we think, would you agree that it is important to be aware of the things we think?

"Whether you think you can or you think you can't," said Henry Ford, "you are right." Our thoughts and attitudes are among the few possessions that are totally ours; not only can they never be taken from us, but we can completely control them. It is only when we continually exercise control over our own thoughts that we can manage external circumstances. Real change comes from the inside first, and our behavior naturally follows.

The Winning Feeling

So, how do you overcome that unsuccessful thinking? How can you replace it with a winning feeling? The one simple secret is to change your unconscious creative mind. How does one do that, you might wonder? Again, the answer is simple. Most truth is. Although it is simple, it will take time, commitment, and a little bit of faith, but the results might amaze you!

First, you begin by picturing exactly what you are attempting to achieve. Let's assume your goal is financial success. Start by imagining in your mind's eye what that looks like. If you had already achieved tremendous success, what are you doing today, now that you are successful? What are your appointments for the day? Will you be sailing your 200-foot yacht in the Caribbean, or skiing down the Alps, or enjoying a leisurely day around your estate? Get the picture? What does it look like? What are you driving, and wearing, where are you going?

Once this picture is imagined clearly, now describe how it feels. Can you feel the gentle Caribbean breeze blowing your hair and cooling your skin? Or, are you feeling the exhilaration of skiing down the slope of the mountain, the chill of the fresh mountain air in your face? Or, rather, are you feeling a peaceful, relaxing calmness as you lay in your lounge chair along-side your Olympic-size pool? How does it *feel?*

The winning feeling itself does not cause you to operate successfully. It is more like a thermometer, which does not cause the heat in the room, but measures it. However, we can use this thermometer in a very practical way. Simply define your goal or end result. Picture it in your mind clearly and vividly. Then capture the feeling you would experience if the desirable goal were already an accomplished fact. Thus, you are geared for success.

There is truly magic in this winning feeling. It can seemingly cancel out obstacles and impossibilities.

Great Motivational Books for More Inspiration

Think and Grow Rich by Napoleon Hill

The Millionairess Across the Street by Bettina Flores and Jennifer Basye Sander

The Dynamic Laws of Prosperity by Catherine Ponder

Dream Big! A Woman's Book of Network Marketing by Cynthia Stewart-Copier

The Aladdin Factor by Jack Canfield and Mark Victor Hansen

Get That Winning Feeling!

Are you getting the picture of what that winning feeling can do for you? So, just how big of a difference can your thinking make in your life and achievements? Let me tell you a story about Brad DeHaven, and how when he changed his thinking, he changed his life.

Brad and his wife Kim were a typical young married couple in their twenties, living in Southern California. Kim had a corporate job, and Brad owned his own business. Just starting out in life, they were living paycheck to paycheck, hoping that their fortunes would rise.

When they met Scott and M. J. Michael, their lives changed. Scott and M. J., already successful Diamonds, took an interest in this young couple and began teaching Brad and Kim the principles of success that had made them wealthy.

Now a Diamond himself, Brad likes to tell his audiences how he created a positive mission statement for himself and repeated that statement everyday, replacing his own personal self-doubts with a winning attitude. It does work, and you can do it too!

Definition Please!

Many companies have special terms for achievement and recognition. "Diamond" is an elite level.

Dexter Yager, one of this industry's leaders and most financially successful men, frequently reminds us that thinking big is not only important, it is clearly the most critical step toward your journey to success. He regularly addresses auditoriums filled with tens of thousands of IBOs, not only teaching them how to reach their dreams but also helping them learn the leadership secrets of success. He says that without a dream, nothing happens. If we don't know what we want out of life or this business, how can we develop a game plan of success? Dexter is not the only one who believes this is true. Scientists believe it too.

Your Brain Records Your Life Experiences

Two men, Dr. John C. Ecceles and Sir Charles Sherrington, experts in the field of brain physiology, share that the human cortex is composed of some 10 billion neurons, each with numerous axons (feelers or "extension wires"), which form synapses (electrical connections) between the neurons.

When we think, remember, or imagine, these neurons discharge a measurable electrical current. When we learn or experience something, a pattern of neurons forming a "chain" is set up in the brain tissue. This "pattern" is not in the nature of a physical "groove" or "track" but more in the nature of an "electrical track"—the arrangement and electrical connections between various neurons being somewhat similar to a magnetic pattern record on tape. The same neurons may thus be a part of any number of separate and distinct patterns, making the human brain's capacity to learn and remember almost limitless.

These patterns are stored away in brain tissue for future use and are reactivated or "replayed" whenever we remember a past experience. In short, science confirms that there is a "tattooing" or action pattern in your brain for every successful action you have ever performed in the past. And, if you can somehow furnish the spark to "replay" it, it will execute itself, and all you'll have to do is "let nature take its course."

When you reactivate successful action patterns out of the past, you also reactivate the winning feelings that accompanied them. By the same token, if you can recapture that winning feeling, you also evoke all the winning actions that accompanied it.

Make Yourself a Treasure Map!

Bring your dreams into sharper focus with a treasure map. Set aside an afternoon and grab your magazines, scissors, and glue. Start cutting out pictures of the things that will surround you in your new, prosperous life. Don't hold back now—cut out the picture of the new Mercedes you will drive, the tropical islands you will visit, the plush cashmere sweaters you will wear. Paste these inspirational pictures on a big piece of cardboard—your treasure map! Sounds corny? In fact, the clearer the vision of what it is that you want to achieve, the greater the chance you will achieve it! Not to mention, it is great fun to spend an afternoon with scissors and paste!

Build Success Patterns in Your Brain

I once read a speech given by Charles William Eliot, A.B., former president of Harvard University, on what he called the "Habit of Success." He said that many failures in elementary school were due to the fact that students were not given, at the very beginning, a sufficient amount of work at which they could succeed and thus didn't develop the "Atmosphere of Success." The student who did not experience success early in his school life found it more difficult to develop the Habit of Success—the habitual feeling of faith and confidence in undertaking new work.

He urged teachers to arrange work in the early grades to ensure that students experience success. The work should be well within the ability of the students, yet interesting and challenging enough to arouse enthusiasm. These small successes, said Dr. Eliot, would give the students the feeling of success, which would be a valuable ally in all future undertakings.

We each can acquire the Habit of Success by following Dr. Eliot's advice to teachers. If we are habitually frustrated by failure, we are apt to acquire habitual negative feelings that color all new undertakings. But by arranging things so that we can succeed, we can build an atmosphere of success, which will carry over into larger undertakings. There is much truth in the saying, "Nothing succeeds like success."

Play Back Your Own Success Patterns

Everyone has at some time or another been successful. It does not have to have been a big success. It might have been something as simple as standing up to the school bully or winning the sack race at the office picnic. It might be the memory of your most successful business deal. What you succeeded in is not as important as the feeling that came with it.

Remember how great success felt? All that is needed to foster more success is to be able to call up some experience where you succeeded in doing what you wanted to, and something that brought you some feeling of satisfaction.

Go back in memory and relive those successful experiences. In your imagination, revive the entire picture in as much detail as you can. In your mind's eye, see whatever accompanied your success. For example, if you had set a goal of getting rid of 20 extra pounds and you hit that goal, remember in detail everything that surrounded that success. What sounds were there? Were you at the gym or in your home when you stepped on those scales and realized you had made it? What did your surrounding environment look like? Who else was there? What else was happening around you at the time? What objects were present? What time of year was it? Were you hot or cold? And so forth. The more detailed you can make it, the better.

Try to particularly remember your feelings at the time. If you can remember your feelings from the past, they will be reactivated in the present. You will find yourself feeling self-confident because self-confidence is partially built on memories of past successes.

Inspire Yourself!

My friend Jennifer has a great way to stay upbeat and inspired, regardless of what is going on in her life right now. Carry one of those tiny little tape recorders with you and give yourself a motivational boost whenever you need it. Turn on the tape and in your most upbeat voice, record messages that you can play to yourself throughout the course of the day, messages like: I DESERVE TO SUCCEED! I GO FOR IT! MY LIFE IS CHANGING FOR THE BETTER EVERY DAY! MONEY AND SUCCESS COME EASILY TO ME! EVERYDAY IN EVERY WAY I AM GETTING BETTER AND BETTER! Create your own slogans to repeat throughout the day. You'll be amazed at what a difference it can make in your attitude and energy level. Give it a try.

Now, after arousing this general feeling of success, give your thoughts to the transformation speech, business deal, or whatever it is that you wish to succeed in now. Use your creative imagination to picture to yourself exactly as you would act and feel if you had already succeeded.

Positive "Worry"

Mentally, begin to play with the idea of complete and inevitable success. Don't force yourself. Don't attempt to coerce your mind. Don't try to use effort or willpower to bring about the desired conviction. You don't have to begin by trying to force yourself to have absolute faith in the desired success. This is too big a bite for you to mentally digest—at first. Begin to think about the desired end result as you do when you worry about the future. When you worry, you do not attempt to convince yourself that the outcome will be undesirable. Instead, you begin gradually. You usually begin with a "suppose." "Just suppose such and such a thing happens," you say mentally to yourself. You repeat this idea over and over to yourself. You play with it. Next comes the idea of "possibility."

"Well, after all," you say, "such a thing is possible." It could happen. Next comes mental imagery. You begin to picture all the various negative possibilities. You play these imaginative pictures over and over to yourself—adding small details and refinements. As the pictures become more and more "real" to you, appropriate feelings begin to manifest themselves, just as if the imagined outcome had already happened. This is the way fear and anxiety develops.

Cultivate Faith and Courage

Faith and courage are developed in exactly the same way, only your goals are different. If you are going to spend time worrying, why not worry constructively? Begin by outlining and defining to yourself the most desirable possible outcome. Begin with your "suppose." Suppose the best possible outcome did actually come about? Next, remind yourself that, after all, this *could* happen. Not that it will happen, at this stage, but only that it *could*. Remind yourself that, after all, such a good and desirable outcome is *possible*.

You can mentally accept and digest these gradual doses of optimism and faith. After having thought of the desired end result as a definite possibility, begin to imagine what this desirable outcome would be like. Go over these mental pictures. Ply them over and over to yourself. As your mental images become more detailed, you will find that, once more, appropriate feelings are beginning to manifest themselves, just as if the favorable outcome had already happened. This time, the appropriate feelings will be those of faith, self-confidence, and courage—all wrapped up into one package: that winning feeling!

Overcome the Bad with Good

Feelings cannot be directly controlled by willpower. They cannot be voluntarily turned off like a faucet. If they cannot be commanded, however, they can be wooed. If they cannot be controlled by a direct act of will, they can be controlled indirectly. If we cannot drive out a negative feeling by making a frontal assault upon it, we can accomplish the same result by substituting a positive feeling. Remember that feelings follow imagery. Feeling coincides with what our nervous system accepts as "real" or the "truth about environment." Whenever we find ourselves experiencing undesirable feelings, we should not concentrate on the undesirable feeling, even to the extent of driving it out. Instead, we should immediately concentrate on positive imagery—filling the mind with wholesome, positive, desirable images, imaginations, and memories. If we do this, the negative feelings take care of themselves. They simply evaporate.

If, on the other hand, we concentrate only on driving out worry thoughts, we necessarily must concentrate on negatives. And even if we are successful in driving out one worry thought, a new one, or even several new ones, is likely to rush in—since the general mental atmosphere is still negative.

I spent much of my youth with my grandmother, Jewel. Many precious lessons of life were learned while working beside her in the kitchen or garden. The best piece of advice she ever gave me was to practice positive mental imagery—immediately and "on cue," so to speak—whenever I became aware of negative feelings. When challenges presented themselves before me and I began to feel those overwhelming feelings of defeat, I would immediately remember my grandmother's words and replace those negatives with positive thoughts and feelings. Negative feelings were literally defeated by becoming a sort of "bell" that set off a conditioned reflex to arouse positive images in my mind. Through years of practice, I now teach my children these same success principles that my grandmother shared with me long ago. It works!

It's Your Choice

Each one of us has a vast mental storehouse of past experiences and feelings—both failures and successes. Like inactive recordings on tape, these experiences and feelings are recorded in your brain. There are recordings of stories with happy endings and recordings with unhappy endings. One is as true as the other. One is as real as the other. It's your choice which one you select for playing back in your mind.

Another interesting scientific finding about these patterns is that they can be changed or modified, somewhat as a tape recording may be changed by "dubbing in" additional material or by replacing an old recording with a new one simply by recording over it. The patterns in the human brain tend to change slightly each time they are "played back." They take on some of the tone and temper of our present mood, thinking, and attitude toward them. This is not only very interesting but also encouraging. It gives us reason to believe that adverse and unhappy childhood experiences and traumas are not as permanent and fatal as some psychologists would have us believe. Not only does the past influence the present but also the present clearly influences the past. In other words, we are not doomed or damned by the past. The old can be changed, modified, or replaced by our present positive thinking.

The concept does carry a responsibility, however. No longer can you derive sickly comfort from blaming your parents, society, your early experiences, or the injustices of others for your present troubles. These things may and should help you understand how you got where you are. Blaming them, or even yourself, for past mistakes, however, will not solve your situation or improve your present or your future. There is no merit in blaming yourself. It's your choice!

Like a broken tape player, you can keep on playing the same old "broken record" of the past, reliving past injustices, pitying yourself for past mistakes or failures—all of which reactivate failure patterns and feelings of failure, which in turn color your present and your future. Or, if you choose, you can put on a new record and reactivate success patterns that conjure up that winning feeling and that help you do better in the present and promise a more enjoyable and successful future.

Change your mental imagery, and the feelings will take care of themselves. Then you will truly be able to *think big* and grow your business to the level of success you dream about!

CHAPTER THREE

Build Wealth by Owning a Business

So, now I've got you thinking big, *really* big, about just where you can go in life. And you know that you can get there under your very own power. You know how dangerous it is to just drift through life on automatic pilot. Deep down you are more than ready to believe you *do* have what it takes to reach your goals.

As you know, we can establish goals in so many areas: family goals about how we want our children to behave, where we want them to be educated, and where we want to raise our children; personal goals having to do with our own appearance, weight goals, or exercise goals; even travel goals (I'm sure I'm not the only one who keeps a list of the places in the world I want to visit in this lifetime).

But let's look at one very specific goal: wealth creation. The title of this book—*Creating Wealth on the Web with Quixtar*—contains a very big goal, and I'd like to devote this chapter to talking about the many ways that wealth is created in this world. As you know, there are many more ways to create wealth now, in the twenty-first century, than there were in decades past. We'll examine them all, but first let's take a hard look at the way that wealth is seldom created.

Wealth is seldom created by working for others.

That's right, wealth is seldom created by working for others. Read on to find out about what two best-selling authors discovered about the very rich, or what can happen to someone who devotes years working for a large corporation. Or even what might be in store for employees who hope that company stock options will rewrite their futures.

How Not to Grow Rich

"If only I could get that big raise," you think to yourself, "My family and I would be on easy street." Is this something you might say? Do you believe that if only someone else would pay you the money you deserve to make, your troubles would be over? If only your salary were higher, then you could pay your bills, buy that bigger house, and sleep easier at night. . . .

I hate to burst your dream, but real wealth is seldom built by working on a salary for someone else. Wealth is built by building your own business.

What the Stockbrokers Know

A recent internal survey that brokerage house Merrill Lynch conducted to learn more about its own customers revealed a fact that you must learn from. Merrill Lynch discovered that fully 70 percent of their high-net-worth customers—the folks who had assets of $5 million or more—owned their own businesses.

Merrill Lynch did not discover that their high net worth customers were well-paid executives with stock options. Their high-net-worth customers were not folks who inherited money. Their high-net-worth customers were not folks who struck gold investing in high-flying Internet stocks.

Seventy percent of their customers with assets of $5 million or more owned their own businesses.

It sounds like such a simple formula. To build wealth, build a business. But building a business can involve so much money, so much time, so many headaches. And so millions of people stay away from starting a business, working instead to make someone else rich.

All Those Millionaires Next Door

It's not just the brokerage house Merrill Lynch that recognizes the fact that so many high net worth individuals are folks who started their own businesses; bestselling authors know it too! Two college professors, Thomas J. Stanley and William D. Danko, spent the better part of 20 years researching wealthy folks: who they were, where they lived, how they made their money, even down to what kind of car they drove. Several years ago, they compiled their findings into a bestselling book called *The Millionaire Next Door: The Surprising Secrets of America's Wealthy.*

What did they find? They found that most American millionaires were pretty ordinary folks; in fact, they were the very folks that you might never suspect were worth that much money. These people lived modestly, in

Who Gets Rich in America?

Merrill Lynch discovered that most of its high-net-worth clients owned their own businesses.

The authors of *The Millionaire Next Door* found that two-thirds of American millionaires have their own businesses.

Who gets rich? People with the desire, drive, and dream to take advantage of an opportunity and build a business of their own!

basic houses, drove older model American cars, and were still married to their original spouses.

What else did they find? They discovered that the overwhelming majority of millionaires made their money by *owning their own businesses*—not by being paid a lot of money to work for someone else, not by taking a flyer on a hot new stock, not by inheriting money from a rich relative (as a matter of fact, according to the authors of *The Millionaire Next Door*, 80 percent of America's millionaires are first-generation rich).

Here are the exact findings of Stanley and Danko regarding who becomes a millionaire: self-employed people make up less than 20 percent of the workers in America but account for two-thirds of the millionaires.

Pretty convincing fact, wouldn't you agree? It seems clear that to control your own financial destiny, you must build your own independent source of income.

The vast majority of Americans millionaires operate their own independent businesses.

High Salary—High Risk?

Bringing in a high salary is a tremendous feeling of accomplishment and satisfaction. Someone else is recognizing your knowledge, your skill, your talent, and is paying you accordingly. Week after week you smile as you revel in the size of your paycheck.

You build the big house, you send your children to private school, you set aside part of your money to invest. You are doing everything right. Until someone else—that someone else for whom you've been working—pulls the rug out from under you. It happened to Stephen Heinrichs. . . .

For 20 years, Stephen worked for a large California food processor as a critical member of the management team. For 20 years he received promotions and raises, accolades, and pats on the back. He was an important member of the team, and he was treated that way. "I thought this was a job I would retire from," he told me.

But Stephen saw that the business was changing rapidly, and that in order to stay competitive, the company that he worked for would have to change too. "Industries change over time," Stephen explained, "and you help make the changes, you recommend the changes. It is all a part of being management."

Then one day Stephen's supervisor called him into his office. "You've been recommending changes for five years now, and it is my duty to inform you that you are part of that change." Stephen's well-paid corporate job was over, just like that. He was shown the door after 20 years of company loyalty.

As he looks back now, Stephen cautions other corporate employees like himself that what happened to him, "illustrates that regardless of where you are, if you are sitting in the wrong chair at the wrong time, that chair disappears. It also impressed upon me that dedication to a company is only so good as long as they need you; how long you need the company is immaterial."

Stephen and his wife experienced a rude shock when they least expected it, and they have vowed not to go through that again. Their plan? They are hard at work building a Quixtar business! They know that to control their own future, they must create their own wealth.

Stephen's advice to those of you who are unsure if starting your business is right for you: "If you want to ensure that you always have an income, you have to work for yourself. And, even more important, if you want to ensure that there is not a ceiling on how much you can earn, you have to work for yourself."

Stephen is by no means the only well-paid executive to lose his job. Just a look at the business section of any newspaper will give you a glimpse of managers in motion, high-ranking people being shown the door. Sometimes experienced folks are being replaced with younger employees who aren't paid as much. The business world can be a harsh one.

But, on the other hand, the message we are all getting from the media is meant to make us relax and take a corporate job. We know how easy it is to feel safe these days. Newspapers and magazines are filled with stories about how low the unemployment rate is right now and how difficult it is for companies to fill their ranks with qualified workers. We hear how the workers they do have are being showered with perks to keep them from leaving: leased BMWs for signing an employment contract, or the ability to bring your dog to work. It seems like an employee's paradise out there.

But does this mean that *your* job is secure? That your salary will continue to climb? That you are safe from ever losing your job? No. Just like Stephen Heinrichs observed earlier, if your company is going through change (and what company isn't!), you stand a chance of being the one looking for a chair when the music stops. And your chair may be missing.

Your paycheck, your life, your family's well-being all depend solely on someone else. It might be the "guy upstairs" (the business owner), the company board of directors, or the shareholders. Your job is secure only as long as you continue to build wealth for someone else.

When you work for someone else, you are not in control of your own financial destiny.

Years and Years of Medical School

Among America's professional class, doctors and dentists are often envied. Years of hard work and little sleep during medical school are soon transformed into flourishing practices, big houses, and country club tee times. But does this still happen? Or are well-educated professionals just as nervous about their long-term income ability as their blue-collar cousins?

Many members of the medical field have encountered the harsh new world of managed health care and have decided that this isn't why they went to medical school—for less money, less decision making, and more red tape and bureaucracy.

Medical professionals also depend heavily on their own physical ability in order to do the job they are trained for. Surgeons must have nimble, flexible fingers. Dentists must be able to stand over their patients for hours on end to peer inside of mouths. But what happens to these folks when their bodies give out? Their incomes give out as well.

In my own Quixtar organization, I have a retired dentist who lost the use of his fingers in a boating accident. How could he possibly keep practicing? He couldn't. Thankfully, he and his wife had begun to build up an independent business of their own before tragedy struck. Despite his medical disability, he had kept his options open and expanded his own ideas of what he was capable of.

Underwater Options

Still not convinced that building your own business is the way to build wealth? That maybe you should get a job with a sexy new high-tech start-up instead? You could work for just a few short years and retire on your stock options, perhaps?

You might be shaking your head in disbelief and saying, "Hey, I've read the newspaper stories. What about all of those folks out there who are rolling in stock options? All of those Microsoft millionaires, those young kids who work for Internet start-ups and drive BMWs right out of school. *They* are building wealth working for someone else!"

Are they? For a while it was certainly true—millionaires, on paper that is, were being created in many high-tech and Internet companies. I call them "paper millionaires" because in most cases their wealth only existed on paper.

These employees were receiving stock options, which gave them the right to purchase shares in the company they worked for at a predetermined price. Options can really pay off when the value of the stock has risen far above the "strike price" of the options, that is the price the employee has to pay to buy the stocks. The employee can then pocket the difference.

But most of the "paper millionaires" were not able to cash in their stock options for months or years. And by the time they could, in many cases the stock price had sunk. The same newspapers and magazines that trumpeted the rise of these young paper millionaires now carry stories of unhappy and depressed employees whose stock options are now "under water," worth less than the current stock price. At the time of this writing, the situation looks bleak, and stock prices for most of those companies are unlikely to rise again to their dizzying heights.

The future of these stock prices could certainly change once again, but the fact remains that these are folks who are not in control of their financial destiny. Far from building their own businesses, they cast their lot with businesses whose fortunes are tied to the whims of the stock market. Some win big, but even more lose big.

Stock options can pay off, but are unpredictable and not as dependable as developing your own income stream by owning a business.

Who Builds Businesses?

Who are the people that build businesses? We've already learned one thing about them from the Merrill Lynch internal survey—they are more likely to end up with a big net worth than are non-business owners!

But what kind of people start businesses and go on to build wealth? Many business owners are folks who have recognized the power of those principles I laid out in Chapter 1, Build Your Dream Business.

Tired of working every day and being paid by the hour? Have you realized that you only have so many hours to "sell"? You might be at the perfect point to try to build a business that can help you escape the time-for-money trap. Many business owners are folks who realized the beauty of doing work just once and then being paid for that work over and over again. These are people who saw that their hourly or salaried jobs were simply time-for-money traps, and so they escaped.

Business owners are often people who are dedicated to building something that they can pass on to their children. Will your children be able to inherit your salaried position at Company X? Most likely not.

The Family Way

If you built your own business, your children would learn valuable lessons about life from watching you in the process. They would be able to learn business skills at your side as they grow into adulthood, and then join with you to build the business even bigger if they wish. Some of the most successful Quixtar IBOs are husbands and wives whose adult children have grown up and joined the business. There are many examples of multimillion dollar families like the Storms and the Florence families. Don and Ruth Storms have been joined in their business by their adult children, Lee, Gail, and Brenda, along with their spouses. Billy and Peggy Florence were delighted when their two children, Hope and Rich, decided to join them too.

These families are able to travel together, to build large and comfortable houses near one another, to relax and enjoy plenty of free leisure time simply enjoying each other's company, rather than experiencing the stress and constant worry that can accompany the life of a salaried employee. They spend time together working toward a common goal, rather than spending time away from their families while working for someone else. And these Quixtar families enjoy working with one another, building their businesses even stronger so that future generations can also inherit this lifestyle.

Let's meet one such family: Don and Ruth Storms own an 18,000-square-foot home on 17 acres of gorgeous country property. They take great delight in entertaining their grandchildren there—a favorite activity is sliding down the 100-foot water slide that winds through the garden and empties into a swimming pool. When the Storms family is not in the country, they and their children and friends can be found on the vacation island they own on the East Coast.

Business owners are often folks who want to build something of substance to pass on to their families and share in a way that a salaried position does not allow.

Old Money

Speaking of families who build businesses, let's take a look at one of the incredible advantages that today's families have over past generations. How were some of the famous family fortunes created in earlier centuries? American fortunes were made in a number of ways: for the Rockefellers, oil; Carnegie, steel; DuPont, chemicals; and Ford, automobile manufacturing. And in Europe, one thinks of the Rothschilds for the family fortune they made in banking.

These names have echoed through the halls of business for decades. But these families and their vast fortunes did not appear overnight. In most cases, it took years of struggle and defeat to ultimately hit upon the one business idea that then allowed them to prosper. These families invested millions of dollars in factories and manufacturing plants, in building banking institutions, and in traveling the world to scout out new sources of materials. These were not easily made fortunes.

Things have changed greatly since those days. Improvements in transportation, business systems, and technology have greatly speeded up the time it takes to build a big business. Businesses can now be built online, on the Internet, without all of the traditional costs involved in starting a company. In the past, to begin building a family fortune you needed to already have one to start with!

To build a lasting business with a healthy income stream, you don't have to start a steel mill, you don't have to develop a software company. You can build a business that takes advantage of the tremendous edge that technology has given us over past generations.

Rich Rewards of Running Your Own Business

Have I got you convinced that you need to escape the time-for-money trap and leave your life as a wage earner or salaried employee behind? Or do you still need more information to help you see that the life you need to embrace is the life of an independent business owner? Let's look at some of the other very real benefits you will experience as you build your own business:

- **Dependable income.** Remember the example of the well-paid corporate employee who received an unexpected pink slip? If you build your own business, no one can hand you a pink slip.
- **Increased self-confidence.** Imagine the pride you will feel when you start to see financial rewards as a result of your own hard work and dedication to your own enterprise. No one told you to do it, you aren't acting on anyone else's orders, you have taken matters into your own hands and have built something of substance!
- **Build your family fortune (instead of others'!).** You can teach your children the rewards of hard work and give them the tools they need to succeed in life through your own example, all the while creating an income stream that could go on for generations.
- **Control over your time and life.** No longer will you punch a clock or sit in a tiny cubicle. Build a home office that fits your personality. Arrange meetings that fit in with your family life. Take vacations that suit your needs not someone else's schedule. Ahhh . . . Lifestyle!
- **The chance to help others build a business.** Unlike the businesses that are built upon the backs of their employees, you

have a chance to build a business that allows you to grow and prosper by helping others to grow and prosper as well!

A Day in the Life

You already have an intimate knowledge of what your everyday life is like in your current situation. Let's take a peek at what your life as a successful IBO might be like. I'm going to describe my own life here, just to give you a glimpse at what I enjoy about the Quixtar lifestyle.

Mornings are a leisurely affair. Instead of rushing everyone out the door on my way to an office, I enjoy breakfast with my children and get everyone off to school before heading off to the gym. After a round or two on the Stairmaster, it's back home to start making telephone calls from my home office. I check e-mail, send my replies, and get caught up on what is happening in my downline and what is new in my upline. I head out to a local café to have lunch with a prospect, and then finish up the afternoon with more phone work. After picking the kids up from school it's time to play and supervise homework.

Sometimes I'm able to combine time with my children with work time. More than once I've found myself on the sidelines of a Little League game, making telephone calls in between watching the action and cheering my children on.

Night times can also be busy meeting times. I meet with prospects and show them the plan, help folks in my downline give meetings, or spend time motivating IBOs. I also spend plenty of time celebrating the success and achievements of fellow Quixtar IBOs!

The choice seems so clear: Why spend your life working toward building wealth for someone else when you can build wealth for yourself with a business of your own?

The Speed of the New World

Definition Please!

A "downline" refers to everyone you have registered. An "upline" is the person (or persons) who registered you.

Those famous families mentioned earlier took many years and many millions of dollars to erect the manufacturing systems and factories upon which their businesses ran. But today, the business scene is light-years away from those days of yore.

It is now possible to build a very profitable business without a factory, without an office tower, without even a desk if you so chose! Read on to learn more about how the development of the Internet and the rise of electronic commerce (e-commerce) have combined to give you the ultimate business opportunity.

CHAPTER FOUR

E-Commerce Explodes on the Web

After reading through the first three chapters of *Creating Wealth on the Web with Quixtar*, I hope you are thinking the following:

> "Yes! I am ready to get involved in a dream business!"
> "Yes! I am ready to start thinking big!"
> "Yes! I believe that the best way to build wealth in my life is to own my own business!"

Are you with me so far? I'm hoping that your heart is starting to beat a little faster, that you're starting to feel enthusiastic, from all of the information I've been giving you. Perhaps your mind is starting to expand and open up to the new ideas of today's business world.

Now, I didn't mean to frighten you in the previous chapter when I described some of what is happening in the job world. Trying to stir someone to action by scaring him will backfire every time. Fear is certainly not the way to motivate someone toward success. But I did want to point out how little control you have over your income and your lifestyle when you are an employee. And I did want to open your eyes as widely as possible, the better that you might see the opportunities that life holds. My intention was to open your mind to receiving the ideas that can bring personal success: to open your mind to the idea that you can truly build wealth for yourself and your family by building a business of your own, rather than working endlessly for someone else.

But you might also be thinking, "Gee, I'm not sure I understand all of this Internet stuff. How can I build a business on the Web? It sounds time-consuming and really expensive."

So let's take a closer look at what is happening online, and you can see for yourself just where the dollar signs are pointing.

Life B.C.—Before Computers

Think back. Think really hard now . . . can you remember life B.C.? Life before computers, that is? Our lives were vastly different then, even as recently as two or three years ago. What little time wasn't spent at work or taking care of children was devoted to an endless round of small errands and time-consuming phone calls to straighten out the kinks in our lives.

I know how much my life has been changed by computers, and by the Internet. I'm guessing your life is different now as well. Instead of searching through the house for a newspaper listing of movie times, or waiting endlessly on hold for the recorded information, I can just hop online and find out what time the newest Disney movie is playing at the theater down the street.

Instead of driving from store to store in search of the perfect going-away present for a long-time friend (and then going through the hassle of finding a box, wrapping it for shipping, and taking it to the post office to stand in yet another line), I can sit down in front of the computer in my robe and slippers and browse through a few Web sites to find that gift and arrange for it to be shipped directly to her.

By logging onto my computer and making a purchase, I've just participated in what is now known as "e-commerce," or electronic commerce. Instead of getting into my car, driving all over town, and spending hours trying to accomplish something, I've just spent a mere 15 minutes and can now spend my valuable time doing something else. This, as you might imagine, is a life-changing development.

Just a Click Away!

Shopping online saves you time and energy! Stop rushing here and there to store after store, looking for that perfect gift. With a click of your mouse the world is at your fingertips!

Let's look at another scenario. Instead of looking at a day in the life of a Quixtar IBO, this time we'll visit the day of an ordinary American online. We'll look at how behavior has changed, and then we'll look behind the computer screen to see who is making money from their new lifestyle habits. And once you understand this new direction that business is heading, you'll begin to see how you too can get a piece of this billion-dollar e-commerce business.

Another Day in the Life

Tom Jones and his wife Sally had big plans for Saturday night—a romantic dinner for two, a babysitter for the kids. But before they could dress up and go out, they had a long "to do" list in front of them. Tom was getting ready for a business trip the following week, and Sally was behind in her household shopping. Years ago it would have meant a day spent in traffic trying to get to the mall, the travel agent, the cosmetics counter. Instead, they just fired up the home computer and logged onto the Internet.

Tom logged directly onto the airline site and typed in his destination and his travel dates. In seconds, the screen showed the best prices and times available. Tom chose one, entered his credit card information, and printed out the electronic ticket confirmation. Task accomplished.

He also needed to restock some of the office supplies in his home office: printer paper, a new color cartridge for his printer, and a supply of presentation folders. Tom surfed over to the Web site of a large office supply company and quickly found what he needed. The Web site confirmed that his delivery would arrive that Monday and that the shipping charge was free. Another long trip in the car was avoided!

Just like Tom's sudden need for printing paper, Sally needed to restock the household with toilet paper, paper towels, disposable diapers, and baby wipes. And she'd noticed that she was running low on her favorite skin cream.

Tom finished his online chores and gave up the seat to Sally. She immediately went to her favorite baby supply site. Diapers and wipes were in plentiful supply, and her choices were soon made. The big bulk items like toilet paper and paper towels, along with her skin cream, were found at the online store of a large drugstore. Sally remembered another quick chore; she also needed to get a birthday present for her nephew's third birthday. She surfed through one or two sites before settling on an educational video.

Time consumed by these tasks? Thirty minutes and her "to-do" list was done. Tom and Sally had the rest of the afternoon free to spend with their children before their big date that night.

Who Made Money Here?

Millions of people like Tom and Sally are on the Web 24 hours a day, buying whatever suits them, whenever it suits them. New e-commerce sites, devoted to everything from booking travel to buying specialized collector's items, crop up everyday.

And those e-commerce businesses, the ones with the Web sites that are selling their goods directly to the consumer, are making better profit margins than ever before. Why? Because they are selling directly to the consumer, instead of wholesaling their product to a retailer, maintaining a fleet of trucks to ship it across the country to the account, and wait 30, 60, or 90 days for the retailer to pay the bill. The high-tech jargon word for this is "disintermediation."

The middleman is disappearing, and when this happens profits go up. So the airline that sold Tom a ticket made more money because it didn't have to pay a travel agent a commission, or even print a ticket! The office supply store made more money because it didn't have to ship product from the main warehouse to a store and then wait for a customer to come to the store and buy it. It shipped directly from its warehouse to the customer.

Who made money here? The big companies who own and operate the commercial Web sites. But, as an independent business owner with a Quixtar affiliation, let me put it another way: It could have been you.

Wow! Can You Get a Piece of This Action?

Yes, you can get a piece of the action with a Quixtar business. Let's look at that day in the life again, this time as an online Quixtar shopper.

Instead of going to several different parts of the Web, Tom and Sally could have logged onto Quixtar, typed in their IBO number and their private password, and they not only could have finished their cyberspace chores quickly but also saved money and earned themselves a bonus as well!

Tom could have gone straight to the travel agency section of Quixtar and booked his ticket. He also could have booked his hotel and car rental at the same time. He could have booked the family cruise vacation, or rented a holiday condominium. And at the end of the month, Tom would have seen a bonus check from the purchases he needed to make anyway! Both save money and make money—what a concept!

And what about his office supplies? While on the Quixtar site, he would have clicked on the Office Max link, made his purchases, and once again seen it reflected in his monthly bonus check.

Could Sally have used the Quixtar site for her purchases? Why, of course! All of her household items, like toilet paper, diapers, and napkins, could be set up to arrive on a schedule that she determines—weekly, monthly, how ever often she needs them. Again, it saves her the step of having to even order them again! Her cosmetics and skin creams? Right there on the site, from Artistry Cosmetics, one of the biggest brands in the business. Shampoo, toothpaste, contact lens solution, coffee, and pet food—it's all here. And all of these purchases add up in your monthly bonus check.

What about the gift for Sally's nephew? Instead of surfing through two or three sites, Sally could have clicked through Quixtar to the Toys 'Я' Us site, bought the video, and once again paid herself in the process.

Think about the power behind not only your own purchases but also those of the people in your organization. It can add up quickly, and you will see it every month in your bonus check.

The Facts and Figures

Let's take a close look at the facts and figures about e-commerce, and where the experts think it is going. I want you to understand the opportunity you have to join this growing business sector.

Back in the dark ages, say around 1989, there were only 100,000 computers with an online connection. It was a pretty specialized thing, mainly involving academics, hard-core computer geeks, and national security agencies. Using the "World Wide Web," as it was called, for commercial transactions was illegal.

But things have certainly changed. Less than a dozen years later, the World Wide Web has morphed into a huge online bazaar, with some 100 million online household users in the United States and Canada alone and nearly 200 million users worldwide. Industry experts predict these numbers will continue to increase in the years to come.

Who is online and what are they buying? Here's who's online—*men, women, and children*. And here's what they're buying—*everything*!

They are buying books, for one thing. You probably recognize the name Amazon.com, the big online book retailer. And online shoppers are buying CDs, airline tickets, movie tickets, specialty gift items, perfume, cosmetics, clothing, even groceries.

Women are online in huge numbers. According to Marleen McDaniel, the CEO of the Internet portal Women.com, 50 percent of the people online are women, and those women account for 60 percent of online purchases.

So, if you could build your own dream business online that appealed to busy families and helped harried mothers save time shopping for household items, would it work? You bet it would! The facts and figures say so.

But Will Online Shopping Continue to Grow?

Are you worried that you have arrived at the online shopping party a little too late, after the best of the hors d'oeuvres have been eaten, and all the cool people have gone? Is it too late to start building a Quixtar business because everyone online has already chosen a favorite shopping site? Heck no!

This is a habit that will only continue to grow. Let's think for a minute about the way you live your life. When was the last time you stood in line at the bank waiting for cash? You just use your ATM card now, don't you? But remember how strange it seemed at first, the idea that you would conduct most of your banking business with what looked like a video monitor in the side of a bank wall? At first, it was just the brave few who gave it a try, and then a few more people got the courage, and now . . . we don't even remember a time when the idea seemed foreign or frightening.

Technological advances and innovation have combined to give us all more control over many parts of our lives, but still so many of us shop the same way our parents and grandparents did decades ago. As more of us begin to question this mundane and time-consuming aspect of our lives, the idea of shopping for what we need online, and having it delivered to our door when we need it, will seem as natural as whipping out the ATM card to pay for a tank of gas.

Building an Online Business the Hard Way

Have I convinced you of the dynamic business possibilities on the Web? Great, let's get started then!

Okay, here is how you start your own online e-commerce business: First, you come up with a wacky idea, spend a few hundred dollars to register your URL (the part that comes after the www.), now start spending thousands and thousands and thousands of dollars to build a Web site, stay up late at night to program the pesky thing, run your credit cards to the max, purchase product to sell and find a warehouse to store it in, figure out a marketing and advertising scheme ("Hey, how about using a sock puppet as a spokesperson?"), take advantage of all of your friends, alienate your loved ones, and . . .

Oh, this wasn't what you had in mind was it?

The "dotcom" lifestyle we've all read about in the press is pretty frantic. We envision a bunch of young people who stay up late at night, eat a lot of pizza, sleep under their desks, and then snowboard whenever they have the chance. It is pretty much the antithesis to what most families want, the crazy hours, the all-consuming focus. It would wreck your family life pretty quickly.

No, the beauty of becoming a Quixtar IBO is that you'll be able to take advantage of the technological possibilities of the Internet, without the disadvantage of trying to start up your own Web company from scratch.

It's So Easy!

As more of us begin to question this mundane and time-consuming aspect of our lives, the idea of shopping for what we need online, and having it delivered to our door when we need it, will seem as natural as whipping out the ATM card to pay for a tank of gas.

The Famous Flames

Recent newspaper stories have trumpeted the online failure of some big-name companies. Disney backed an online toy retailer, called Toysmart.com, and then shuttered it less than a year later. Boo.com, an upscale Swedish clothing retailer, flamed out quickly, burning millions of dollars that investors had poured into it in an effort to make it work.

Many more such shakeouts will occur, largely because of the huge cost involved in developing an online brand name and attracting customers to your site.

But as you'll learn in the next chapter, because Quixtar is based on a "high-tech, high-touch" model, those business-crushing costs simply don't occur. The independent business owners themselves provide the word-of-mouth advertising for Quixtar (rather than, say, a million dollar Super Bowl ad), and the sales just continue to grow.

It is estimated that the cost of developing a name brand (a name like Cap'n Crunch or Coca Cola, one that most households will recognize) from scratch is over $100 million. That's kind of a large barrier between starting up your own "dotcom" and making it big on your own, right?

But Quixtar isn't faced with those kinds of costs due to the strength, numbers, and commitment of its IBOs. This puts Quixtar in a class far ahead of the companies—even big, well-funded companies—trying to make it on the Web.

My Smallsite.com

Oh, this e-commerce stuff sounds exciting, doesn't it? But, you might be asking yourself, should I really become a Quixtar IBO? Maybe I can just build a quirky site with personality and then sign up with some of the affiliate programs that the giant Web retailers run? Those programs are all over the Web: sign up to become an Amazon.com affiliate and make 15 percent, or add a link to an online bank and get a commission every time someone opens an account through my site.

Maybe you can start a chat room for frustrated corporate employees, "cube dwellers," and then add links to a big retailer like OfficeMax.com and make a small commission each time one of your visitors buys a ream of printing paper. Sounds like the perfect home-based business!

The idea is appealing. But the reality is that not very many small Web site operators are making a living from their affiliate links.

The operator of one popular travel information Web site recently revealed that for every 1,000 people who come by his site, he makes about $2 from Amazon.com. Forty-five thousand folks visit his site every month, and he makes $90 from the travel books that they buy. Imagine, if you were a Quixtar-affiliated IBO who had 45,000 visits a month!

Another downside to operating a small site with lots of affiliate links is that each one of these affiliate programs has a minimum amount you need to generate before they will send you a check. Yes, customers might be headed off to the other site from your site, but unless your account reaches $25, the affiliate site won't send you a check. Is that something you want to keep track of? And let's not forget what's happened to the dotcoms recently!

Surfing for Money

Do you have friends who want you to "get paid to surf the Web"? There are huge online advertising businesses that pay ordinary folks to add a banner to the bottom of their home page so that whenever the computer user is online, they are being paid to view the banner. And many of these programs do have a network marketing element to them—get your friends to do it too and you get a fraction of a cent when they sign up and go "surfing."

Millions of folks have joined these programs, and millions were unhappy in the summer of 2000 when one of the most popular programs announced that they would now be paying people less than they'd originally announced.

The *Wall Street Journal* reported that while most program users made under $50 a month, one fellow and his wife made as much as $900 a month from the surfing activities of the 5,000 recruits. Five thousand recruits? And he was only making $900? Imagine if you were a Quixtar IBO with 5,000 people in your downline!

If you are going to ask your friends to join in on a Web venture with you, why not ask them to do something that has the potential to pay a real income, a growing income, an income that could allow you and your family to live the way you've always dreamed?

Building Your Online Dream Business

So instead of surfing for dollars, instead of chasing down small checks from 20 different Web sites, instead of starting your own high-flying "dotcom" business and perhaps wrecking your family life, why not try this instead: point, click, shop, and earn. How much simpler can it be?

In the next few chapters, you will learn all about the opportunities available to independent business owners affiliated with Quixtar. You will be astonished at the difference between what has typically been available in the world of e-commerce, and what is now available through Quixtar.

Surf for dollars by viewing annoying banner ads? Nope. Invest money, time, and heartache building your own small Web site with the hope that someone will find it and buy something from you? Nope.

Instead, become a part of an exciting Web-based earning opportunity from a first-class company with decades of experience and billions of dollars of sales under its belt? You bet!

Sales Will Rise and Rise

It is worth repeating: projections for online shopping continue to grow. When I wrote this book in the summer of 2000, the Commerce Department reported retail e-commerce sales of $5.3 billion in the first quarter of the year. That's 5.3 *billion* dollars! I confess, the number makes the hairs stand up on the back of my arms, imagining that I have the chance to build an independent business that could be an active contributor to that number.

Don't miss your chance to feel included in the action too.

Ready to Meet the Quixtar Opportunity?

So let's put this fast-paced (and sometimes bewildering) world of Internet commerce aside for a moment, while we delve into the opportunity to build up your own income, to truly create wealth on the Web with an online dream business.

CHAPTER FIVE

Meet Quixtar

I know I've piqued your interest about Quixtar with the last few chapters, dropping a few hints about what Quixtar is and what it does but never really spelling it out in detail. Well, now it's time to get down to the business at hand and learn all about Quixtar and how it can help you create wealth on the Web!

Are you motivated? Yes, you are!

Are you ready to build a business of your own? Yes, you are!

Are you interested in learning how Quixtar can help you do that? Yes, you are!

So join me now as I take you on a tour of a real dream business—Quixtar.

What Is Quixtar?

Quixtar, Inc., (pronounced quick star), the new Web-based venture featuring the convergence of shopping, member benefits, and business ownership, rang up more than $250 million in sales in its first 200 days, continuing a torrid pace that should place it among the top five consumer shopping sites in its first year. For serious independent business owners, e-commerce is creating an exciting path to financial success into the new millennium.

Launched on September 1, 1999, Quixtar is reporting daily sales averaging more than $2 million and had its first $3 million day on February 29, 2000. It took Amazon.com *more than four years* to accomplish what IBOs created in the first few months of opening the new digital destination site Quixtar. Visionary IBOs are setting a new standard of excellence in e-commerce. This unprecedented growth is phenomenal by any standard.

Overcoming Obstacles in a Quick Start

Certainly this success did not happen without many setbacks. Statistics compiled by *PC Data Online* show that in just its second week, Quixtar was ranked fifth among all Web shopping sites worldwide when measuring page views. According to *PC Data Online*, Quixtar logged more than 800,000 unique users generating more than 52 million page views for the week ending September 11, 1999.

Challenges are common in any new Internet launch and, unfortunately, Quixtar faced them as well. The initial unprecedented rush to the site, in addition to some technical difficulties, resulted in a few frustrations early on. With five times the projected volume, Quixtar users across North America became frustrated by their inability to log on to the site. Being unable to access their site meant Quixtar would soon be out of business. "Within days, however, we fixed most of the glitches and balanced loads across our 70 servers," said Randy Bancino, Quixtar's chief information officer. "But as quickly as we resolved challenges, the unprecedented traffic continued to increase and challenge our server farm."

A team of engineers from Quixtar and Microsoft quickly installed eight backup server units and deployed an additional 16 high-powered Compaq servers, bringing Quixtar's infrastructure up to more than 90 Web, data, and application servers. In order to stay ahead of the incredible demand, Quixtar also began negotiating with outside companies for regional Web hosting facilities around North America.

"We're committed to the success of this new business and are extremely grateful for the patience and understanding our IBOs have shown. They are our key partners in this venture and without them we never would have seen this kind of response," said Ken McDonald, senior vice president/manager director of the North American Business Region. To reward their patience and recognize their importance, Quixtar increased by 10 percent the bonuses they earned on business volume for September.

"Building Quixtar has been a great adventure for everyone involved," said McDonald. "Most experts predict that e-commerce is the future of business, and we're thrilled to be a part of it. We believe there is no limit to how big Quixtar can become."

That sentiment rings clearly throughout the Quixtar world as leading IBOs continue to sing its praises. Jody Victor, second generation Crown, told me one afternoon, "We may seem to move a bit slower than most, but we are surefooted! Sales on the site are good and getting bigger and bigger. There is no end in sight to the potential we have with Quixtar."

Definition Please!

"Crown," like "Diamond," is a mark of high distinction and achievement.

How Big, How Fast?

It took Amazon.com, one of the e-commerce industry leaders, more than four years to build its business up to the size that Quixtar achieved in just four months. From the launch day of September 1, 1999, Quixtar daily sales averaged $2 million dollars a day; it hit the first $3-million-dollar day late in February 2000.

How It Works

Quixtar is an Internet-based business where affiliated IBOs can register others to be IBOs, members, or clients, thereby earning bonuses on the business volume generated by their activities. IBOs do not have to make the large capital investments often required to launch an online business; to register with Quixtar as an IBO costs $99.95 (U.S., includes $70 worth of products). Quixtar membership costs $19.95 (U.S.), with benefits including special member prices on individual product purchases and "Q Credits" that can be earned through purchases and redeemed for valuable merchandise or converted into frequent flier miles. Clients pay no registration fee and will go to Quixtar for high-quality products and information leading to solutions for everyday problems about their health, home, and other challenges.

"After nearly a year of planning and development, Quixtar's technical dream team has created a site that is functional, fun and easy to use," said Bancino. "We're very proud of the work everyone was able to accomplish in a very short period of time."

The Internet Business Group, a highly skilled development team comprised of about 30 professionals, was assembled nearly a year ago to drive the design and construction of the Quixtar site. Partnering with some of the top developers in the e-commerce business, this team oversees planning, creative design, development, testing, implementation, and maintenance of all e-commerce, Web-based and PC applications, employing leading-edge technology.

The Development Team

Microsoft Corporation
Fry Multimedia
IBM Corporation
Vignette Corporation
C-E Communications/tdah!
Compaq Computer Corporation

"Even though we've been able to hire some very talented individuals to work on this project, we needed to assemble an even larger team that could put this site together quickly, allowing us time to test and tweak prior to our September 1 launch date," said Randy Bancino. "We've brought together the most experienced technical, creative, and interactive firms to join us in developing Quixtar."

"Quixtar recognizes that some of the most important work in electronic commerce goes on behind the Web site," said Towney Kennard, vice president, e-business enablement services, IBM Global Services. "We're providing services to ensure the information systems support the quality customer service Quixtar's customers depend on. We're proud to be involved with a project of this scale."

Quixtar-affiliated IBOs benefit from sales made at these partner stores as each purchase earns points toward their monthly bonus checks. Quixtar members, who are essentially preferred customers, receive "Q-Credits" for each purchase made at a partner store, which can be redeemed for merchandise or frequent flier miles from top airlines.

IBOs and Quixtar members aren't the only ones benefiting from this arrangement. Partner stores have reported significant boosts in sales and traffic, thanks to their affiliation with this emerging Internet giant.

Norbert J. Schneider, president of the Fuller Brush Company, said orders are up at his site because of traffic generated by Quixtar.

"Fuller Brush is a true believer in the impact of Quixtar-affiliated IBOs on e-commerce," said Schneider. "The 144 percent increase in online orders and 180 percent jump in hits we've experienced since becoming a partner store demonstrate Quixtar's selling power."

Partner Stores

Although the list always changes, here are some of the recent partner stores on the Quixtar site:

- Toys 'Я' Us
- Hickory Farms
- Ocean Essentials
- Office Max
- IBM
- Catalog City.com
- Lens Express
- Network Solutions, Inc.
- Franklin Covey
- Gateway Computers
- Diamond Jewelers
- Bass Pro
- Paul Fredrick Men's Store
- FloraGift
- . . . and more!

Ask yourself—isn't that awesome selling and purchasing power something that you want to be a part of?

For some of its partner stores, Quixtar has quickly become their largest account. FloraGift's president, J. Scott Aemisegger, said Quixtar is generating more business for them than even the U.S. military, another large customer. "Quixtar-affiliated IBOs are like nothing we've ever seen. Their drive, energy, and focus make Quixtar our most valuable account," he said.

Quixtar shoppers are also more likely to buy than simply browse, according to WebClothes president/CEO, Jim Anderson. "Quixtar-affiliated IBOs have delivered Internet shoppers that are 2.5 times more likely to make a purchase than our non-Quixtar shoppers," Anderson said.

At CatalogCity.com, holiday-season shoppers entering from Quixtar ordered from more than 90 percent of the site's available catalogs. CatalogCity.com president and CEO, Lee Lorenzen, said his company knew long before the holidays how important Quixtar is to their business. "When we launched, Quixtar's high volume prompted us to add servers and more than double our capacity," said Lorenzen. "Thanks to Quixtar-affiliated IBOs, we were ready for the holiday traffic."

As Jody Victor puts it, "We are available to the public 24 hours a day, seven days a week. We don't have to have operators to take calls and you are never put on hold! Just think, how many times a day does someone in your family stop at the store? The research firm Forester says at least one time per day, often by more than one family member."

Online Success Measures

Web sites are measured by two different methods—the number of unique visitors that come to the site on a daily basis, and the "stickiness" of those visitors. It is meaningless to have huge numbers of people log on and look at your front page. You need to get those visitors wandering from page to page on your site, looking at merchandise, and buying it. You need people to "stick" on your site instead of losing interest and clicking on to another part of the Web.

That simply means that an IBO can create an income 24 hours a day, seven days a week. Are you beginning to see how powerful this business can be for you?

What's the Secret?

The biggest kicker is the way that this incredible growth has evolved. This colossal success has happened with absolutely no advertising. People are wondering how Quixtar pulled it off. They all want to know the secret.

Well, readers, you know the secret don't you? The secret is the independent business owner that I've been talking so much about. It's the personal touch that IBOs develop with their prospects that makes the difference—through phone calls, one-on-one meetings, and group training seminars, IBOs are creating the magic in e-commerce.

And you have a chance to become one of these high-energy people!

"The personal touch provided by nearly 400,000 independent business owners affiliated with Quixtar is the difference between this company and other Internet start-ups," said John Parker, Quixtar's director of business operations. "In six months, we've paid out more than $75 million in bonuses and rewards. We believe our early success demonstrates that the high touch approach is more effective than traditional advertising."

Key drivers to Quixtar's success are the business-building efforts of IBOs and the site's ability to create community, sustain the interest of shoppers, and provide world-class service. Nielsen/Net Ratings recently ranked Quixtar as the seventh "stickiest" shopping site accessed by Web surfers from home.

So, what does all this mean for me, you ask? It means big money in your pocket! According to an industry giant and Crown Ambassador, Dexter Yager, "The success in Quixtar is not just a cool Web site, not just great products and neat partner stores, it is the communities that you, the IBO, build. That is what sets us apart from other e-commerce sites. We have a loyal community of people, committed to their own businesses. It's the IBOs that make this business work."

Consider This!

In Quixtar's first six months of business, they paid out an astonishing $75 million dollars in bonuses and rewards to their IBOs. What did it feel like to get a piece of that action? I can tell you, because my husband and I received some of those checks!

Imagine this: In the morning, I can sit down in front of my computer, still dressed in my slippers and robe, log on to my online bank, and check my account to see if my latest bonus has arrived. And when it has, there is no finer feeling! To watch the size of my account increase month by month, and know that it is due to my own efforts as an IBO, how much better does it get?

And it is much more than the money or the size of my account—I have experienced bonus trips with my husband and children that cannot be measured in dollars and cents. My husband and I earned a trip to the Caribbean and we took our kids along. My children and I held hands as we snorkeled along the coral reef, looking in the crystal blue waters at the spectacular colors of tropical fish. Seeing the delight in their eyes as they spotted yet another one was a remarkable event in my life. The rewards are endless.

A Foot in the Past, a Step Toward the Future

A key to building a successful e-commerce business is to utilize some of the basic principles of building a business. Three-way calls, personal contact, one-on-one meetings, and group training are more important now in this new venue than perhaps ever before in the history of network marketing. Forward-thinking IBOs need to hold on to some of the traditional methods of business while reaching forward

How Does Ditto Delivery Work?

Let's take a look at your typical day. Do you spend countless hours thinking about trivial matters like "Is there enough toilet paper in the house?" "Do I need to restock the baby's diapers?" "Gosh, we are almost out of our favorite cereal, I'll have to stop off at the store on my way home tonight." And once you think of all of the teeny little things you need, you then have to take the time out of your day to go pick up all of that stuff.

But what if you could arrange for all of the staples that you and your family use to arrive at your doorstep every few weeks? Better yet, what if you never had to run to the store to pick up those one or two items? What a timesaver. That's the beauty of ditto delivery!

for the excitement and experiences of the new world of e-commerce.

For example, most of you have walked across a stream or river. Remember how you did it? You probably jumped from rock to rock, attempting to avoid the chilly waters below. But would you jump to the next rock without first putting out your foot to test the security of that next step? No. You stood on one rock, trying to maintain your balance while gently touching the next rock with the tip of your toe, adding pressure until you were confident that the next step would hold you and not drop you into the cold water. Your business is much the same. As you hold on to the proven principles of success from the past, you test the next rock, the new opportunities in this Web-based business. With feet firmly planted in the security of your past success, you have a stable foothold to make the next step into the future.

A Strong Foothold for Success

Helping business owners who are newcomers to e-commerce establish a strong foothold for success is vital. Quixtar currently offers hundreds of brand-name items at its Store for More site and thousands of products at more than 70 partner stores, ranging from OfficeMax.com, IBM, and ToysRUs.com, to Lens Express, Hardware.com and HickoryFarms.com.

But, the best bet for reaching the higher bonus levels is still in core-line consumables, those necessary products we all use every day. Most smart business leaders will tell you that unless you get people immediately on the core-line products that Quixtar offers, you are missing the boat, and so are the people you bring on board. These products give you the greatest profit margin and the higher bonuses—more bang for the buck. Business owners should establish their foothold with core-line consumable products, then step out to the partner stores—thus holding on to the old while building the new.

One of the features helping Quixtar achieve record sales levels is its "Ditto Delivery service." More than 100,000 ditto delivery profiles have been created, allowing Quixtar to provide customized service to its regular shoppers. Ditto Delivery Service allows Quixtar-affiliated IBOs, members, and clients to create personal profiles that result in monthly direct shipments of preselected products based on their projected use rate. Users can also change their profiles at any time.

More Than Your Household Goods

But the success of Ditto Delivery is not just about products, according to Quixtar's Ken McDonald. Quixtar provides its users much more than products. For example, IBOs can find a doctor, research specific disease and health concerns, ask questions, and even learn cosmetic application on a cool "virtual face" link. "We provide more than just products," says Ken. "There's a lot of value-added information there; the total customer experience with Quixtar is significantly enhanced. We're pleased with the growth we've experienced in such a short time," says McDonald. "We're seeing tens of thousands of new people each month as our IBOs spread the word about Quixtar and what it offers as a shopping site and Web-based business. We're looking forward to considering significant expansion in the not-too-distant future."

By utilizing Ditto Delivery, a new business owner learns an important first step toward financial success and gains the experience to teach and duplicate this standard to his newest downline. Often, that new IBO will hit a higher bonus level on his or her first day and will learn how easy it is to get that first bonus check. You better believe the excited IBO won't be able to wait to share that same opportunity with others!

Stepping Forward

Getting a new business owner to step off the shore toward success is also critical. With e-commerce, this important journey begins with a touch of leadership and mentoring. "Leaders need to help all business owners become familiar with this new way of doing business and help them understand how to get off to a fast start toward success. Building a solid relationship of trust has never been more critical in this new era of business," says Don Storms, Triple Diamond with Quixtar.

Without that personal touch, your new business partner might lose his balance and slip. Helping him make a safe journey to solid ground is crucial in the beginning. Whether through three-way calling, satellite broadcast training, or home meetings, investing time by guiding him through his first orders, helping him develop a large contact list, advising him through those initial calls, or offering help for meetings will build relationships that will carry that newest person across the rocky path to success.

"Lot's of folks thought that with this new business model, there would not be a need or a demand for business seminars or support material. This couldn't be farther from the truth!" adds Don Storms. "Personal and business development has never been a more critical component in development of a successful business as it is today with Quixtar."

Don Storms says that Dexter Yager taught him about the value of books, audio and videotapes, and training conferences. Don says that these are the tools for a duplication pattern for success that is the touchstone for creating synergy and momentum. And the high touch it provides can equate to bigger bonuses for the IBO. Dexter Yager told me that this system of success, taught by industry leaders for many years, is the same system of success that will sky rocket new business owner's e-commerce businesses in this new millennium.

In the next few chapters, we will return to these themes of how to develop an organization of other IBOs and keep them motivated and building their businesses.

Crossing into the Future

While Quixtar opens the door to newer and bigger opportunities for the future, principles of success don't change. As you move from a traditional network marketing business into a new e-commerce business, it is much like crossing a stream. You keep one foot on your proven principles of success while moving forward with e-commerce. What made network marketing great to begin with is what will propel the Quixtar business to success.

PART TWO

Dare It!

CHAPTER SIX

Eight Simple Steps to Success, Part One

Are you with me, now? Yes, you need to build your own business in order to control your financial destiny and achieve financial freedom. Yes, you have a handle on what is happening on the Web with e-commerce and why this is a great time to get involved. Yes, Quixtar sounds like an incredible opportunity to achieve that financial freedom. But how, exactly, can this happen? Is there something, some step, some action that comes in between deciding that you will become a Quixtar-affiliated IBO and achieving your financial goals? Yes. It's called hard work. Planning. Follow-through.

No army ever fought a battle, no architect ever designed a home, and no football team ever won the big game without a well-defined plan. A well-defined plan is essential in achieving success. This chapter will outline your step-by-step pattern, a game plan to follow toward financial success, toward the fulfillment of your dreams.

Hundreds, thousands, possibly hundreds of thousands of other successful IBOs have used this pattern for success. It works, and if you use it, you will find success easier and faster than if you try to develop what I call "the idea of the week," business ideas that come fast and go just as quickly. Why waste precious time trying to

How Important Is a Plan?

How many significant achievements have ever been accomplished without a plan? Did Churchill have a plan to fight the Germans? Yes. Did NASA have a plan to land a man on the moon? Yes. Did Microsoft have a plan to grow their business? Yes. Did Oprah have a plan to design her show? Yes. Start now to work on your plan to achieve financial independence for yourself and your family!

develop a game plan when this plan is already a proven success? If you thoroughly learn and implement this pattern for success, you will build a faster, stronger, more profitable and duplicable business.

You may be wondering, "Can I do it? Can I learn how to develop a profitable business in this new Internet world?" You bet you can! Just follow these eight simple steps and teach others to do the same, and your business will skyrocket to success.

Let's begin with Part One, the first four steps!

1. Define Your Dream

Do you truly know what it is that you want out of life? Is it sharp and clear in your mind? Can you close your eyes and picture it down to the way the flowers in the bountiful garden of your dream home will smell? When he first started reaching for his dreams, motivational master Mark Victor Hansen could. He planned his garden—the fruits and vegetables he would grow, the scent of orange blossoms that he would pass on his way through the gates of his oceanside estate. It was all clear in his mind. And he got it! One of the things he wrote down was that he wanted to become a best-selling author. Ever heard of the *Chicken Soup for the Soul* series?

Yep, he got that dream, too. Writing down your goals and dreams is a powerful tool for action.

In the absence of clearly defined goals, we push forward in life, sometimes aimless and misdirected, often working hard only to discover at the end of the day or year that we are unsatisfied and unfulfilled. Where did the time go? How did we let those minutes, hours, and weeks slip by? Where did we go wrong? So many folks go wrong in one significant way—they never take the time to define their goals and dreams.

The clearer your goals are, the greater your chance for achieving achieve them. It isn't magic, it doesn't simply happen on its own. By writing down your goals, you are creating a master "to do" list for your life. Mark Victor Hansen has achieved hundreds of the financial and personal goals he set for himself, and then went on and thought up thousands more! You need to constantly challenge yourself to achieve.

I live in California, where there is a state lottery system. Every week, millions of ordinary folks go out and buy tickets in the hope that they will be the big winner, that they will look down at their ticket and see the magic numbers that will lead them to the easy life. And I know you've played this mental game before too . . . "If I won the lottery, the first thing I'd do is . . ."

See, you do have some sort of a vision about what you would do with more money in your life after all! So write it down. Don't be embarrassed. Don't be shy. Write it down.

Okay, I know I sound a bit like a schoolmarm here, but I do want to give you a writing assignment. It could prove to be the most powerful, life-changing, thing you have ever done. I'd like you to stop reading this book for 15 minutes and perform this exercise: pick up a piece of paper and start giving shape to your goals. Start defining your dreams.

I know you can do this. I know that you can picture the exact kind of car you'd like to own someday (and hopefully someday when you are still spry enough to drive it!). No doubt somewhere in your mind is a list of the things you'd like to be able to provide for your children: a college education, private tutoring, or European vacations. And somewhere in your mind are things you'd like to do someday with a loved one: weeks of sunning on the beach in Hawaii, evenings spent in Parisian cafes, long lazy days driving an RV around to all of the national parks.

What else do you want from life? To pay off your mortgage early? To spend more time with your children? To write the great American novel? You have the desires, you just need to put them down on paper.

As you write out your desires, be as specific as you can. Instead of specifying "a trip to Paris," write "two weeks with my spouse at the Hotel Ritz in Paris." You can *see* that much better, can't you?

Once you feel more comfortable writing things down, why not honor your dreams and goals by writing on fancy paper, or placing your dreams in a gilded box. Coauthor Jennifer Basye Sander likes to write her goals and dreams down on stationery from swanky hotels. If you don't happen to have any lying around the house, you could go to her motivational money site (*www.goalsandjewels.com*). It has blank financial goals forms you can print out for yourself. But whatever you choose to write your goals down on, just make sure you do it! And by adding pictures of your goals, you will be able to "see" them, to completely visualize them, and create the image in your subconscious mind that these things can really be yours. And if it's motivation you need, go to *www.DaretoDreamBig.com* and sign up for your weekly dose of motivation.

I recently listened to Jack Canfield, Mark Victor Hansen's partner on the Chicken Soup series, talk about how he stayed motivated toward achieving his goals. While describing his own path toward achievement, Jack made an interesting observation: *That if we set our goals high enough and continually strive to achieve them, we will become better people in the process of working to achieve them*. The very process of trying to achieve the goals we have set for ourselves improves us! It polishes our rough edges and expands our knowledge; it opens our hearts and minds to the world around us and helps us reach out to others. Why wait? Set the highest goals you can think of!

Remember, writing down your dreams and goals is the first step toward making them come true.

The Extra Payoff

Setting goals, working hard, and finally achieving those goals is an extraordinary accomplishment. It gives you an incredible glow of achievement. But there is more to it than mere achievement! Not only do you get to accomplish your goals—whether they be personal, financial, or business-related—but also chances are that along the way you have actually become a better person. By going through this process, you will have learned new skills, made new contacts, increased your confidence, built up your ability to help others, and otherwise transformed yourself for the better! Congratulations!

2. Make a Commitment and Develop a Plan

Nothing worthwhile in life is obtained without commitments, although sometimes it seems that people are afraid of them. They can be scary for two reasons: (1) We are afraid that they won't be able to fulfill us, or (2) We're scared that we won't be able to fulfill them. Often, people shy away from commitments because they already know how awful it feels to be committed to projects they don't believe in, job titles they don't enjoy, or relationships they've outgrown. A conclusive, clear-cut, definitive decision is often the singular element that separates the winners from the losers. Plans change—commitments don't.

To make your dreams a reality and achieve the balance and lifestyle you seek, you must first make good decisions. Wise decisions are vital to the fulfillment of your dreams. For example, if you desire to be an NBA player, you should turn down the offer for a cigarette. If you want to do undercover work for the FBI, don't involve yourself in any illegal activities. If you want to be accepted to a particular college, you find out what its requirements are and decide to exceed them.

CREATE A GAME PLAN

Armies never go into battle without a plan. Coaches don't send players into a game without clearly outlining the plays. Chefs don't begin preparations for a great meal without first checking the ingredients and recipes. And you can't start down the road to success without a plan, either.

Every choice you have ever made has had an influence, however slight, upon your path in life. You are who you are and where you are today because of countless choices that you've made during your lifetime. You can choose to be cheerful or you can choose to be sad. You can choose to be rude or you can choose to be courteous. You can choose to love your neighbor or you can choose to hate your neighbor. You can choose to be prosperous or you can choose to be broke. When you understand that every choice has an end result, you place yourself in a position to become successful in every area of your life.

Every choice that you make takes you either toward what you want in life or away from your heart's desire. In Chapter Two, we discussed defining your goals and dreams—determining what your personal driving force will be. In this chapter, we will be defining what your plan or strategy will be to attain those goals and dreams.

Now, you will get focused on the course that will get you heading down the right path.

MAKING A COMMITMENT

When someone says to me, "I'll try," I know that I can't count on him or her. Trying is the lowest level of commitment, just a noisy way of not doing something. There is a vast difference between being involved and being committed. When you are "interested" in something, you do it when it is convenient, but when you are "committed," you follow through no matter what—no excuses!

Many people are involved rather than committed. They talk about *trying* to do something, rather than actually *doing* it. I have been working with a trainer at a local gym for six months now. I am committed. However, this was not always the case. There was a time that I believed I was too busy for exercise. I have changed my mind. Although I still have the same 24 hours in a day, my commitments have changed. Exercise is now a priority in my life, and I am committed to doing it. There is a big difference between knowing I *should* exercise and actually *doing* it! An *interested* exerciser wakes up on a rainy morning and says, "I think I'll exercise tomorrow." A *committed* exerciser wakes up to rain and says, "I better exercise inside today."

When a person is committed to doing something, he or she will find ways to suppress excuse making, even when their commitments may be inconvenient at that time. Such a person will keep his or her commitment. Persistence in life is characterized by this mental and behavioral toughness.

COMMITMENT IS CRITICAL TO YOUR SUCCESS

Now that you understand how critical commitment is to your success, have you evaluated your own commitments? Perhaps start with your *why*—your reason for doing something, or for your dreams—then move to your particular business plan, which should not only include your own product line, training system, and support material but also should address your upline leaders as well as your own downline partners. Decide today that you will be in the 100 percent club—that you will be *100 percent committed* to your own business, products, and most importantly to you!

Sometimes people get involved in their Internet business and just seem to "play" at it. They say they want to make big money, yet they treat their business as if it is just a little hobby, something that they can do in their spare time. I wonder if their dreams and goals are just not very important to them—mine were. I spent 40-plus hours a week at my job. "Why would I imagine that I could make serious money in a business of my own if I gave it less effort?" one of the industry leaders told me. I knew that some things in my life were nonnegotiable—my kids, my job. I also knew that some of the other things I gave my time to each day were not really important. I found that doing a few simple things differently every day gave me many more hours of discretionary time each week. I used this saved time to make a life for my family and myself. I worked at my business for a few hours after work and almost every weekend. In just a few months, I had exceeded my income from my day job and within that first year, I was free from that job altogether. Today I enjoy life, my family, and friends, and a decent income is definitely not a problem. I believe that because I stayed consistently committed to my goal, I am able to enjoy such a great lifestyle today.

ON YOUR MARK . . .

Now you are ready to get in the race for success—the race to financial freedom. You know that Quixtar and the e-commerce boom is big, and it's getting bigger. You now know that this is the best business opportunity for making money. You have a list of clearly defined objectives and goals, have made some commitments, and are now ready to get started! What's next, you ask? Well, it's time to get started on another list—of prospective business associates.

Who Do You Know?

"But I don't know anyone," you say? Sure you do! You know hundreds of people who are just waiting to have their lives transformed too. Don't you talk to these people daily? Teachers, mail carriers, grocery checkout clerks, postal workers, package delivery drivers, bookstore personnel, bank employees, neighbors, car pool parents, soccer coaches, librarians, relatives, or hair stylists? Your life is filled with people—and potential prospects!

3. Develop a List of Potential Business Associates

So, here we are at step number three. First you set your goals, that one was great, wasn't it? Then, you made the commitment to move forward with Quixtar. You know that becoming a Quixtar IBO can help you achieve your goals and dreams list. In step three, you will begin to compile a list of prospects, all of the people in your life that you know on a first-name basis.

Let me tell you about how a very successful Quixtar IBO developed her list. Amy Grant is a woman I know well—she is my own upline! Prospecting is a step that is best done in close association with the person who sponsored you. But as Amy explains, "My sponsor lived over 3,000 miles away." Despite the distance, Amy's sponsor sent her the training information she needed to develop her prospecting skills. It wasn't enough for Amy; she was hungry for more.

"I was hungry for more information, and so my sponsor put me in touch with someone else in our upline who had already reached the level of success I was searching for." Her upline helped her jumpstart her business. The first piece of advice: Get to work on the best prospect list you can!

Some people refer to this as a "warm" list, a list of folks from your present and past that you know well enough to pick up and call on the phone, people who will recognize your name. Developing a large warm list can be your first, most powerful engine in your race toward success as a Quixtar IBO.

MAKE IT A BIG ONE

"I was told that to develop a big business, I needed to develop a big list," Amy says. "And I did!" First she wrote down the obvious people that came to mind—folks like her own family, friends she'd made over the years, and coworkers. Dipping a little deeper into her memory banks, she began to recall the names of friends who'd moved away, and former coworkers who'd changed jobs. When those memory cells went dead, Amy dragged out her guest book from her wedding, her old school yearbooks, and even found some old Christmas card lists. She was on her way to a big list and a big business!

Does this sound like it will be hard for you to do? To sit down and start writing down names of people you know? Goodness, another writing project already! Just like writing down your dreams and goals, writing down your list of prospects is a critical step toward achieving success.

"But I don't know anyone!" Oh really? Consider this: Research indicates that by the time an ordinary American is 30 years old that person knows 2,000 people on a first-name basis. TWO THOUSAND? I can hear your skepticism. But it is true. Think about the people in your life—the mailman, the UPS driver, the woman at the local dry cleaning business. Let's keep going here. Do you have kids? Okay, what about their teachers, their soccer coach, or Sunday school leader. And you, what about the lady you buy coffee from every morning? Your hairdresser or barber? You've got to talk about something while you sit there in that chair once a month!

Yes, there is a good chance you do know 2,000 people on a first-name basis, so start writing them down now. Sound like too large of a goal? I'm just trying to set the bar higher so that you will reach for the stars.

One great way to help the names and faces flood in is to use memory joggers. No, I'm not asking you to suit up and go running. I'm suggesting that there are things in our lives that help us remember times, places, and people. Music is great for this. Have you ever heard a song on the radio that brought your high school days flooding back? And when those memories come back, so do the faces and names from that part of your life—the name of the guy who sat next to you in French class, the woman who helped out part time in the library. Write them down!

Help Your People Win!

There are great audiotape series available that can really motivate your downline (not to mention yourself!) Reading positive, self-help books is invaluable when working to develop your own successful business. Reading not only helps you, it helps you teach, train, and develop your people into the leaders of the future. Check out some of these:

The Magic of Thinking Big
by David J. Schwartz

Think and Grow Rich
by Napoleon Hill

Dynamic Laws of Prosperity
by Catherine Ponder

RELATION-SHIPPING

The bottom line in your business is not profit. The real bottom line in this business—the one that will be decide whether you grow or not—is relationships. People relationships, that is, not product relationships. I've heard these words of wisdom over and over in my business career, and I urge you to keep this concept foremost in your mind as you begin making your calls. You aren't in the product business—you are in the people business.

4. Contacting and Inviting

You've written out that big list, you are focusing on your big dream, and now what? Gee, do you really have to call these people? Yes, you bet you do. Will you have the strength to pick up the phone and make those calls? Yes, you will. Because your dream is clear, you will find the strength.

I've talked to many a successful IBO, and every one of them agrees that this is a business in which numbers are critical. Numbers are critical in any business, I know, but what I mean here is that the number of people you contact is critical. What are your numbers? Are you prepared to make 30 to 60 calls a day if that is what it takes to succeed? Sounds a bit scary, doesn't it? But let's look at this another way. What if you knew that there was money hidden under a rock in your own backyard, somewhere although you weren't exactly sure just where it was hidden. So you'd have to go out there and start picking up rocks, peering into bushes, happily spending the time because you *knew that there was money there—it was only a matter of time until you found it.*

Building your business as an IBO is just like this. Yes, your success is right out there—it is only a matter of time until you *find the people who will build up successful businesses with you.* So keep making those phone calls, one after another, just like you would keep picking up those rocks, one after another.

You won't be able to tell who will make it in this business. Nor can you guess who will truly succeed. Sometimes the people most likely to succeed will be the first to quit. And those whom you think don't have a prayer will shoot to the top! So pick up the phone and start making your calls now!

DON'T PREJUDGE

One of the biggest mistakes newcomers make is to try to figure out who *will* do this business and who *won't*. I can almost guarantee you that you simply can't determine this in advance. Many of the top moneymakers in the industry told me that it is impossible to know who will and who won't make it in this business, because winners pick themselves, we don't. So reach out and touch someone. You may never know the impact your initial approach may have in the lives of another person. Reach out to everyone. Don't prejudge.

CONSULT YOUR UPLINE

After consulting with your upline, researching all of your training material, and making a huge names list—start talking. Contact your top 25 people first, and remember to utilize your greatest asset, your upline. I often have new people rehearse their invitation with either me or one of the leaders in my business. Perhaps you could simply call on the telephone, pretending that you are talking to a new prospective IBO. This allows you some time to not only improve your verbiage and approach, but also increase some self-confidence, if you need it. Once you schedule those first few appointments, I suggest that you try to arrange for your sponsor or upline to be there with you for your first two or three meetings. It's best to present the opportunity to small groups of two to 10 people at a time.

Remember this rule of thumb—always invite twice as many guests as you want to attend. You must always allow for the "no-shows," which are an inevitable part of this business. Focus your first 90 days on "*relation-shipping*"—that is, reaching out to those closest to you and extending the invitation to create a business partnership intended to enhance the quality of their lives.

CHAPTER SEVEN

Eight Simple Steps to Success, Part Two

So, you've learned the first four steps to making your business grow and your dreams come true. Now let's look at the next four steps, and then you'll be ready to race to the top and achieve the success you've always dreamed of.

5. Have a Successful Meeting

The first meeting with your prospective partners is critical; it might make you or break you. If it is successful, you will feel energized and optimistic. If it is not successful, you might feel discouraged and disillusioned. So the amount of planning you put into holding your very first meeting is crucial.

Jim and Darlene, both top IBOs, said this was especially true for them. "In the beginning my sponsor helped me to make a list of prospective partners and even helped me make those first few appointments," Darlene says. "I think if I had been left alone to make those calls, I would have put it off. But because I did not want to look silly in front of my sponsor, I had the extra courage to pick up that phone."

New IBOs often tell me that their sponsor motivated their initial success. Helping that new person make calls, or stepping in for a conference call, will give them the confidence and assurance they need to take another step forward. Don't be afraid to ask your sponsor for help. "I thought I had to know everything, be prepared to answer every objection or question, before I could get started," says Jim. "If my sponsor had let me wait until I was sure I could handle everything on my own, I would still be waiting."

Ask your sponsor to help you make calls and set up appointments. And be sure to look to them for added doses of encouragement and the answers to last-minute questions. Jim's sponsor helped him set up his first four or five presentations, but at the same time encouraged Jim that he could easily do this on his own. "He just kept smiling at me and saying, 'you can do it!' For some reason, I believed him." Jim's sponsor also emphasized the importance of preparation. Jim learned that first impressions are key, and he worked hard to make sure that his meetings ran smoothly.

QUALIFY AND CONFIRM

How do you have a successful meeting? An important part of having a successful meeting is confirming that you are, in fact, going to *have* a meeting! New IBOs, in their haste and excitement, often neglect to qualify and confirm their appointments. "In the beginning I was so nervous, so excited that I sometimes forgot to pin down my prospect and confirm our appointment. There were a few times that I showed up and the prospect wasn't home! I had piqued their interest, but forgotten to get a commitment," Jim said. Oops. Don't let this happen to you!

You'll need to determine the level of your prospect's interest. This is called "qualifying." Is your prospect *really* looking for a business opportunity, and is he or she *truly* interested in hearing more about your business plan? Or is he simply being courteous? Asking qualifying questions in the beginning will save you much time and many, many headaches.

Here are some good qualifying questions:

"If I could show you a way that you could increase your income without jeopardizing your current job, would you be interested in getting together to discuss the details?"

"Last week you mentioned that you really wanted to stop commuting and wished you could work from your home. Did you really mean it? Yes, well then I think it would be smart for us to get together. I have some great ideas for a home-based business that I think you'll be excited about."

The responses to these basic qualifying questions help you determine the level of interest. Then you can go to step two: confirming the appointment. When your new prospect expresses a desire to meet, this is your chance to immediately pull out your calendar and ask that she do the same. "Jan, I have my calendar in front of me, do you? I have Tuesday or Saturday open. Which is better for you? Would you prefer 6:00 P.M. or 8:00 P.M.?"

By offering your prospect a choice of two dates, you can have better control over your own calendar as well as get a specific day pinned down. "Okay, I'll be at your house on Tuesday at 8:00 P.M. And I want you to know, Jan, that I am very good at keeping my appointments. Are you?" you ask. As you are confirming the appointment, you then take it one step further. I want my prospects to know that they can count on me, that I keep my word. And I want them to know that I expect them to keep their appointment. By taking just a moment to ask a couple of questions, I have been able to keep my calendar full. And I seldom knock on a door and find nobody home!

THE PURPOSE OF A MEETING?—THE NEXT MEETING

Every appointment I make is with the intention of securing the next one. If I am going to share the marketing plan with a new couple, my goal is to get to the next meeting with them, whether to sign them up, get them started, or simply to follow up and answer their questions. I never leave a meeting without securing an appointment for the next one. This way, my calendar is always full and my time is used more effectively.

REHEARSAL TIME

In Chapter Eight, I will help you develop a method for practicing and polishing your performance. But until then, let me just tell you this:

Rehearse, rehearse, rehearse—in the mirror, to your dog, your neighbor, or an artificial plant. It can be helpful to tape record yourself and critique your own presentation. Work with someone in your upline to smooth out the flow of information and make yourself as confident as possible. Most importantly, start giving presentations!

DON'T PANIC

What is it that we fear the most during our first few business plan presentations? We are all terrified (I know I sure was!) that someone will interrupt us and ask a question. Yikes! Now what? When people begin to ask questions, don't panic. As a matter of fact, you should be pleased! People who ask questions or give objections are at least taking you seriously. Eileen Sargent says, "I learned how to handle objections early in my career. Business on the Internet was exciting to most people, but because we were a relatively new business model, people had lots of questions. I was always happy to get the questions. I knew that meant they were interested and wanted to know more."

A SUCCESSFUL MEETING IS YOURS!

Congratulations, you are ready to hold a meeting! Put your best foot forward by dressing for success and rehearsing your presentation. Then you will present a professional and compelling marketing plan and ask for the sign up. This will move you even further ahead. By inviting your prospects to participate in the presentation and encouraging their remarks, you can easily sell the benefits of your own particular marketing and compensation plan. And most importantly—it doesn't matter as much *where* you hold your meetings—what ultimately counts is *how many* people you talk to about your business plan. As my friend Billy Florence always says, "The one who shows the most plans wins!"

As you learn to hold successful meetings and teach your own system of success, you will be teaching others to teach, thereby creating huge numbers and tremendous volume in your business. By utilizing the council of your upline and learning the power of duplication, you can plug in and power up!

6. Follow Up and Follow Through

This important step starts the first time you meet with your potential IBO. Immediately begin the follow-up by arranging the next appointment. This appointment should be within 24 to 48 hours after giving the business plan to your newest prospect. Successful

IBOs Rolland and Molly Hughes say this is the "honeymoon" period. They told me, "Those first couple of days are critical to your new people's success because this is when they are the most excited, the most positive, and have the greatest level of belief." If you allow too much time to pass by before getting back together, often that new guy will have talked to his neighbor, who naturally knows everything about your business, even though he has never built one himself. Or, more commonly, that new guy will start his own negative self-talk. "I have never been successful in business before. What makes me think I can do this business and make it work?" he may ask himself. Meeting with him again quickly will give you the opportunity to assure him that the dreams and goals he shared with you just a couple of nights ago are attainable in this new Internet business. You can give him hope and let him know that you will be there all the way. He may feel inadequate for the job, but with your confidence and commitment to him, he will believe that he can do it!

EYE TO EYE

The best way to follow up and follow through with your new IBO is to do it in person whenever possible. Eye to eye is by far the best way. "When my upline came back to my house two days later, I could just feel his commitment, to this business and to me," says Quixtar leader, Bob Sargent. "He eliminated all of the fears that I had been building in my mind over the past two days. When I realized that he meant business and he was really there to support me, to support my success, I asked to register that very night."

Instilling the confidence and belief in new people is a critical step toward their success. By getting back together with them in those first important 48 hours, you will sidestep lots of problems. And you will be not only showing them your commitment to your business and to them, but teaching them an important pattern to follow.

7. Progress Check—Review and Report

Progress checks are critical to success in any aspect of life, whether managing a career, developing a lasting relationship, or developing a strong business. Leaders check their progress regularly, first to their own goals and dreams, then to their commitments to others, to their product or service lines, and most importantly to the system their leaders have developed—more specifically submitting a "progress report" of sorts to their upline leaders and mentor.

It has often been said that a chain is as strong as its weakest link. Learning to develop a strong link between business and people—products and upline training systems—will aid you in the development of your Internet business and the financial security you seek. Let's first talk about leadership: what it means and how to develop leadership qualities in yourself.

GREAT LEADERS BEGIN AS STUDENTS

All winners have coaches! They win more consistently than others because they are willing to listen and to put to use the new ideas that their coaches present to them. The same is true with great leaders. First, they were willing to learn, to be good students. With this humble attitude, great leaders are born.

To be teachable you have to want to be better! The greatest coach in your business can't teach a person who is unwilling to learn. Being teachable is learning to listen differently. A lot of people can't handle this one. They have things made up in their mind—they see things in a specific way and that's it! They tend to place restrictions on what they will or won't listen to. They "already know," and, therefore, no one can tell them anything! How sad and limiting! It is a mistake not to look outside the rigid boundaries of our minds.

It can cost you a great deal of money too! As Bert Gulick often says, "Big mistake. Big! Huge!"

When you are teachable, let your leaders know. Tell them that you are requesting their counsel or help. Ask them to tell it like it is, and give them permission to assist you. Let them know it's really okay to be honest with you. Say to them, "I can take it! For me to be able to be the best I can be, I want and need your ideas, opinions, suggestions, and advice. Please say what is on your mind."

MASTER YOUR EGO

The greatest addiction in the world today is not necessarily what you might think—drugs, sex, or alcohol—it is the human ego. The human ego can destroy family life, marriages, and relationships faster and more efficiently than most any other addiction.

Leaders who fall victim to this addiction want to be center stage. They often are threatened by the success of others, so they fail to develop and use people's talents or notice them doing something right. They want to be the best, and the only one being recognized.

A great rule for doing business today is to think more about your people, and they will think more of themselves. And don't act like you are perfect. Leaders need to come out from behind their curtains of infallibility, power, and control and let their "very good" side, their humanity, be revealed. Folks like to be around a person who is willing to admit his or her vulnerability, who asks for ideas, and who can let others be in the spotlight. As Norman Vincent Peale once said, "People with humility don't think less of themselves, they just think of themselves less."

8. Teach the Fast Track Pattern to Others

Look closely at the business signs on any major street corner in America and you will have a sense of familiarity. Haven't you seen those businesses somewhere else before? Like in your own town, on a corner near you? Wendy's, Taco Bell, Burger King—over and over, the buildings and the businesses look the same. Why? What is the reason for the overwhelming success of franchise companies like McDonald's?

The answer is duplication! Duplication works. McDonald's created a simple franchise system that is easy to teach to others. Then they did it over and over again. I have been from Los Angeles to London and the french-fries at McDonald's taste the same!

Don't worry, we don't want you learning how to make french fries. But the point is that by tapping into proven successful money making systems and utilizing the power of duplication, you have the opportunity to create an incredible lifestyle.

Remember, duplicating your upline's pattern for success does not mean you have to imitate them. You shouldn't try to be like another person but rather should take the great qualities and wisdom and incorporate those things into your own personality. By duplicating another's pattern for success, you win!

HELP YOUR PEOPLE WIN

What is the sign of a great leader? Great leaders are selfless people who are deeply committed to helping their people win. In this Internet business, huge success comes only after you have helped others win big. My own upline, Don and Ruth Storms, teach me by their example, and what a tremendous example it is.

Don says he always wants to "kick the newest guy out of the nest," or get them out there on their own, trying and learning and growing their way to success. By leading the way and offering encouragement and support, Don's people begin to realize that they can build a big business; they can duplicate the pattern for success that he has taught them. As they take steps on their own and accomplish success, it gives them the confidence and enthusiasm to do even more—to stretch even further outside of their comfort zones. Because Don and Ruth actually *do* what they teach, it gives others hope and faith. Even the newest business owner might say, "If I follow them, do the steps they teach and duplicate this pattern in my own business, I could have the kind of lifestyle that they enjoy."

What does a real leader do? The main job of a leader is to help people succeed in accomplishing their goals by setting the pace ahead of them. In other words, by *doing* what you are teaching.

You need to be out there prospecting every day if you expect your IBOs to prospect everyday. You need to be giving several meetings a week if you are asking others to do that. Then, when people in your downline learn from your own example and are able to accomplish their goals, everyone wins.

GET REAL

In my last book, *Dream Big,* I talk a great deal about my own upline and mentor, Don Storms. I'd like to repeat some of that here, because I believe that much of my own success stems directly from his help. Everything Don has ever told me has been right. I always know I can trust him and count on him. His integrity is what really drew me to him. Because of my trust in him, I was able to open up, reach higher, stretch further. I encourage you to try to become this kind of a leader. I hope that in the years to come, successful IBOs in your downline will begin to write business books in which they credit you for their success! It could happen.

Who are the mentors in your life? Are you seeking their council and following their advice? Perhaps your mentor will inspire and guide you to make choices and changes in your life that will enable you to reach the pinnacle of success that you dream of. Then you can share that gift with others. Sometimes the greatest rewards in life come by helping others succeed.

Follow the Steps

Recently, my youngest daughter, Rebecca, and I decided to plant some flowers in the yard. As we bent over, our backs toward the morning sun, she asked me, "Mommy, where do flowers come from?"

I started to teach her the creation of the world, but the look on her five-year-old face convinced me to try another approach. "Okay, honey! I'll show you where flowers come from." We jumped in the car and dashed to our local nursery where we poured over racks of flower seed until Rebecca found just the right shade of pink. "This is it!" she exclaimed, as she held up a packet of primrose seeds, with a giant smile across her plump, sun-kissed cheeks. How could I resist? We also bought two pots, some dark, rich potting soil, fertilizer, and a small watering can and took off for home.

I talked about how important the soil and fertilizers are to the growth of our flowers as we dumped the dirt into the clay pots. Rebecca's tiny fingers carefully dropped the precious primrose seeds into the rich dirt, and she gently patted down more soil on top. Then we filled the little watering can, and she slowly covered the soil with a shower of water.

"What's next?" she asked.

"Now we wait," I replied. "Now the sun and water and soil will do its job and the little seed inside will sprout. As the seed grows, it will break through the top of the soil and grow and grow into the beautiful flowers you see on the packet. Of course, we have to continue to water it everyday and make sure it gets enough sunshine, but not *too* much. In a few weeks you'll have your flowers. And that, Rebecca, is where flowers come from."

Evidently satisfied, she skipped off to play inside. As I began to clean up our mess, I thought, "I can't make the sun shine. I can't will the rain to fall. I can't make the soil rich and I can't force those little seeds to sprout. But if I follow the proper steps, I will have flowers."

Just like I couldn't force the seeds to sprout, you can't force people to succeed. You can't make them do the work. You can't fill them with a dream, but if you'll follow these eight simple steps, you *can* grow a prolific business! You *can* grow into a success.

CHAPTER EIGHT

Find the Gold

Now that you've read more about the opportunities that are open to Independent Business Owners, you might be asking some very tough questions: How do I find out more about building a downline? How can I interest others in this opportunity? These are valid questions for sure. Keep on reading, friends, because this chapter and Chapter Nine will give you more of the tools you need to strike gold as a Quixtar IBO. I touched on some of these ideas in my Eight Simple Steps to Success, but here we will examine just one of those steps in detail. Let's take a closer look at the process of "prospecting."

Panning for Gold

Last summer I took my two youngest children to Sutter's Mill. It is a little place off Highway 49 in Northern California, made famous in the mid-1800s when gold was first discovered there. It is an interesting little town, rich with history. As we walked along the shaded dirt paths we talked about how it might have been to live back in those days. My son, Tyler, with all of the confidence of a 10-year-old boy said, "I bet I would have found more gold than anyone in

Finding Gold

Who gets rich in a gold strike? Some of the miners do, some of the mine owners do, but the many people supplying the picks and the shovels make out the best. How can you make this work to your advantage in this new economy gold rush? Decide that you aren't going to be the one who spends millions on developing a Web site with the hope that you'll strike gold with it. Instead, ally yourself with a company that is going strong in the picks and shovels area—a company like Quixtar!

this whole town! I would be the richest guy around."

I told him about the hundreds of men who lost everything they had, even their very lives, in their pursuit of gold. Still eager to strike it rich, Tyler convinced me that we should try our hand at panning for gold, and so we rented a tin pan and after a brief demonstration by a local store-owner, we set out to find our golden nuggets. For several hours we sifted through gallons of water, dirt, and sand, while the hot sun was pounding on our heads and our muscles ached from the strain of bending over the river. After sifting and sorting through mounds of tiny particles of rock and sand, the best I found were several tiny fragments of fool's gold. Tyler ended up being the only one who actually found gold—a tiny nugget, about the size of a pencil eraser.

Panning for gold was a lot of hard work. We had to go through a ton of dirt just to find one small piece of gold. Building a successful Quixtar business is much like panning for gold: you have to go through a lot of people before you find the golden ones, the ones who will really make it big! But when you do find those golden people, you will feel much like my son Tyler did that day at Sutter's Mill when he finally found his gold nugget. He jumped up in the air and exclaimed, "I found one. I found one. We are going to be rich!"

Keep on Panning

Teach your people to keep sifting and sorting. Don't be a fool like many of the early miners were. When they found what they thought was gold they stopped panning, only to discover later that all the gold they had collected was worthless. Don't stop sorting and sifting (sponsoring) until you have found enough gold—enough leaders to make you rich!

The most successful IBOs are those who continue to sponsor leaders, regardless of the size of their organization.

My upline, Leo and Amy Grant, teach their IBOs to register at least two new people a month. Do Amy and Leo practice what they preach? You bet they do! Regardless of the fact that they have thousands of IBOs already in their organizations, the Grants continue to sift and sort, looking for the gold in their new people.

Prospecting Tools

All actions leading to success in this Internet business are based on the strength of your prospecting ability. It is largely a numbers game: the more you prospect, the more you will recruit—and the more your business will grow. If you contact 100 people, you'll recruit far more than if you prospect only 10 people. Prospecting is the foundation and the key to success.

It is vitally important to understand this concept. Many will register one or two "heavy hitters" and then wait for the gold to come in. In my experience, most of these "superstars" are not who they say they are. Some of them will suddenly disappear without even a "goodbye"; others will register 10 people in a day—and then move on to other things; still others will have personal challenges that "request" all of their attention for a while. Any business builder will tell you that they have been disappointed by some promising candidates who delivered little or did nothing at all with the opportunity. It just happens.

What's the preventive cure for this syndrome? There's only one: prospect, prospect again, and then prospect some more. When you have a broad prospecting base, dropouts don't affect the growth of your network; it's simply a built-in factor.

Unexpected Superstars

The other side of the prospecting coin is also very compelling: people you didn't count on will surprise you and rise up to their own potential, becoming super players on your team and propelling you to high levels of success.

In order to build a powerful organization, it is critical to do a high level of prospecting and give a solid start to your new business. Just think: If you contact 1000 prospects in your first 100 days (that's only 10 a day!), you'll create unstoppable momentum and a residual income for life. What else could you possibly do in 100 days that would bring you financial freedom and freedom with your time as well? How many years (or perhaps, lifetimes!) of college would it take to get to that point in life?

What am I suggesting here? It's simple: For a period of 90 to 100 days, go for it—full out! Invite everybody you know to a meeting or a teleconference. Ask your upline for prospecting audiotapes and videotapes. Tell everyone you meet about your company and its benefits. Ask for referrals. Place ads. Prospect everywhere—on planes, trains, and automobiles, at restaurants and parties, at weddings and baby showers—anywhere and everywhere. Don't waste time; cut down on your TV time, romance novels, surfing the Web, perusing junk mail, and any other unproductive activities. Get focused!

When you do the prospecting phase of your business building, do it intensively. Your team players will model your strategy and you'll be on your way to a fabulous experience with your business.

Be Choosy

Selective sponsoring makes good business sense. The most important asset of any business professional is time. In other words, effective time management is critical to success; productivity rather than just plain activity is the idea. Bringing in folks who have little desire for or chance of success, just for the promotional volume and to cut a paycheck, is not only unethical, it means that more time resources will have to be expended to replace those folks who drop out. Continual IBO replacement is ineffective time management.

I look for people who will succeed with or without my help if I can just point them in the right direction—those who have goals, dreams, and the willingness to do whatever it takes to achieve them. With a little support, their achievements may prove to be stellar.

Have you ever heard of the 80/20 rule? Eighty percent of the work is done by 20 percent of the people. This business is no different. When looking for the right folks with whom to share this great business idea, I look for people who are already busy, who are already successful in some aspect of their lives. Perhaps they walk with their heads a little higher, their step a little faster, or their smile a little broader than those around them.

It isn't always the CEO of company XYZ that I look for either. It could easily be a mother at my daughter's school who runs the PTA or the fellow across the counter at the cleaners. I am looking for people with ambition and drive, regardless of their present occupation.

The past 30 years have been a protracted pioneering phase in this industry. From the days of distributor warehousing, before the advent of common carriers, to today's high-tech business mechanisms, one fact has remained constant: this business is still fundamentally built on belief—a belief in the industry, the company, the products, and in one's self. "Can I do it?" is the question of paramount importance to every potential IBO.

My process of prospecting is designed to not only satisfactorily answer that question in the mind of my prospects, but also to instill in them the confidence that their success is a foregone conclusion. Just as the day has come when prospects are starting to interview for the most effective sponsor they can find, as the public wakes up to the emergence of the industry, the day will come when prospective IBOs will wait in line to join quality companies—and there is none better than Quixtar. Let it begin now! Within my organization, it has already begun.

How Do *I* Do It?

Are you with me so far? If you have never done this before, it can perhaps seem strange or intimidating. Let me tell you how I incorporate this into the course of my day, and I believe you will see how it flows quite naturally. At this point, I'd like to give you a clear picture of exactly what I do and say when prospecting for a new member or client. Be sure to check with your upline and find out what he or she thinks may work best.

I often use the third-party approach: "Who do you know that . . ." (would like to be their own boss, spend more time with their family, earn unlimited income, etc.)? My first step is setting an appointment when the prospect asks for more information about Quixtar. I never give any more information than necessary to set up the appointment.

Let's try another example. To the fellow at the cleaners, I might start out like this: "I can't help but notice that every time I come here, you are so friendly and so eager to help. Do you own this cleaners?" He may say yes or no, but either way I will continue: "As friendly as you are, I imagine you must know a lot of people around here. I am expanding my business in this area and am looking for a few people to help me with this expansion. Who might you know that would be interested in making some extra money, either on a full- or part-time basis?"

You'll notice that I don't give him a bunch of information about my business at this point. Am I being cagey, evasive, trying to "trick" him into something? No! I am simply gathering information from him at this point. Why would I share the details with a person before I find out if he is interested?

More often than not, the fellow at the cleaners will respond with, "Well, is there a way for me to make some money too?" at which point I would arrange to meet with him to discuss the details.

Most new IBOs, and even some who have been around awhile, blow their best leads by giving the prospect enough information for him or her to quickly disqualify the opportunity. "I know all about that and I don't know anyone who would be interested," might be his mental reply.

If I can't get an appointment without giving away "disqualifying" information (it rarely happens for experienced leaders, but it is a common occurrence with novice IBOs), my mental reply is "Next!" I'm not in the business of convincing folks to sit down with me to find out how they can earn a six-figure income if they're not interested. I'm in the information-dispensing business, not the convincing business. If I have to sell folks on the business today, I'll have to sell them again tomorrow when their coworkers tell them that they're nuts. Having a little ambition and a desire to improve his or her life is the first quality that I look for in a prospective distributor. Without ambition and desire, everything else is moot.

The first appointment is scheduled for the prospect to evaluate the opportunity to determine if he knows anyone who is qualified for an interview. At that appointment, I set the stage by casually telling the prospect, "I know this isn't for you." This takes all of the pressure off of him. He is no longer concerned that he might be setting himself up to be talked into a business deal. Once relaxed, the prospect is more inclined to listen with an open mind.

I follow up by stating, "I know that you're happy where you are. I'm looking for someone like you (highly motivated, good organizational skills, a self-starter, whatever applies) but who is concerned about . . ." Then I list all of those things that I know he is concerned about in his current situation: downsizing, loss of pension, cut in pay, time away from the family, and concern for the future.

Almost every single time, the expression on the prospect's face changes from one of curiosity to one of despair and anguish as the points that I make, referring to a third party, cause him pain by hitting so close to home. They apply to him also.

Handled correctly, within 15 minutes, the interviewee will usually timidly profess an interest, "What about me?"

My response is a resounding, "You? You wouldn't be interested in this! You're happy where you are!" The more bellicose I am, the better it works. This is big-time take-away. I have now created fear of loss—the only external motivation that works.

Once the prospect starts to explain that he really is interested, I ask him the second most important question of the entire interview. That question, which I ask as if I don't believe it, is "Why would you want to do this?" This question starts a prospect on the process of selling himself on the concern that he has about his existing condition or his future and gets him to verbalize it, thus reinforcing it in his mind. This phase is extremely important. I just let him talk. The longer he goes on, the more animated he will become. If he slows down, I ask questions about his situation, which are designed to bring him back to the direction in which I want him to go. The whole process is designed to bring the prospect to the self-realization that he is living his life like a caged rat.

I then ask the prospect the single most important question of the entire interview. A second interview rests on the conviction of his answer. "What do you really want to do with your life?"

Ninety-five percent of the time the prospect doesn't have a clue. The trick is to trigger in him the realization that, regardless of his station in life, he has allowed himself to become like a mindless hamster on a treadmill. When that realization registers, you can see it on his face.

I'm looking for the tiny spark that says, "It doesn't have to be this way." I'm looking for someone with a desire to change his life. My determination of his desire to take charge of his life and be the architect of his own destiny is pure gut. It comes with practice.

If I don't sense desire and conviction, I know he's not a viable prospect. I accept that I probably won't get any quality leads from him because if he doesn't have the belief in himself to change his situation, he probably won't have the belief in the opportunity to recommend anyone worthwhile. Nor, as a rule, will he likely know or associate with people willing to step up to the plate and accept ownership of their future. I'm looking for movers and shakers.

At this point, I conclude the first interview even though I haven't even shown the plan. If I've

Keep Prospecting!

The journey of 1,000 miles begins with a single step. The network of 100,000 IBOs begins with the single step of prospecting. Keep prospecting—there's a mountain of golden nuggets out there just waiting to be discovered. Stake your claim!

sensed the desire for change, I'll end by saying, "I'm still not sure that this is for you, but I'll tell you what—would you be willing to listen to some tapes? If these tapes help you gain a better understanding like they have for other people, we'll talk again. Let's schedule another appointment now, the sooner the better; otherwise I might get booked up and not be able to get with you for several weeks."

This has gotten a commitment even though he still doesn't know what "it" is. It's important at this point to find a tape that he needs and can relate to or his chance for success is minimal. This is another reason why Quixtar leaders believe in the power of the training system.

If the prospect won't book a definitive appointment, (i.e., "I'll get back with you"), it's a signal that the interest level isn't where it should be, and mentally I drop him off my list. My upline taught me not to dance too long with too few that never really wanted to dance in the first place.

I have seen well-meaning IBOs waste precious time trying to turn these uninterested folks into successful partners. It just doesn't work. Spend your energy with those folks that have a dream, that want something more out of life. It doesn't mean you stop going to that cleaners, change your banking account, or stop being friends with the person who said no. It just means understanding that no means no. Keep moving forward. You'll find your gold!

CHAPTER NINE

Create a Golden Opportunity

The time has come! You've identified a hot prospect, you have an appointment to show her the Quixtar opportunity . . . now "whatcha gonna" do? The stakes are rising ever higher, this is your chance to start building your organization and generating some real income. How can you make sure that you can interest him in becoming a Quixtar IBO?

Suppose you were an actor on Broadway. Would you go on stage in front of your audience without knowing your lines? Would you begin your performance without all of the props being in place and the audience being seated properly? I didn't think so.

Let me ask you this: Is your enrollment presentation just as important to you and your family as a Broadway performance? Do you know your lines? Do you know how to set the stage that will guarantee your prospect's undivided attention throughout your sales performance?

If you're not sure about the answers to these questions, it's time for you to learn (once and for all) how to stage your presentation for maximum performance and results. And as long as I am on this Broadway metaphor, don't forget that there are blockbuster shows on Broadway that have been running for decades, making money every night. Let's get to work and create a long-running success for you too.

In the following examples, I'll continue to talk to the fellow from the dry-cleaning business. Let's assume I will be attending an appointment at his home.

Ten Points for Professional Presentations

1. QUALIFY THE APPOINTMENT.

Why go on a call if your prospect has not indicated a genuine interest in your program to begin with? Not knowing if you have a serious, motivated prospect and still going to an appointment is like rolling dice and hoping you get lucky—*not* a good bet.

Why not qualify your appointment before your meeting by first asking him a question like this over the phone:

"If I can show you how to create a royalty-type income, while allowing you to spend more time at home with your family, would you be receptive to meeting with me to discuss the details of my business?"

How could anyone say no to a question like that unless he was irrational, illogical, unmotivated, or just basically unqualified? And if he comes across to you this way, forget about him. You'll be glad you did.

Let's take a look at my prospect from the dry-cleaning business. Let's call him Joe. He did listen to the tape I gave him and Joe called me back, insisting on learning more. Had Joe not called me, I would have called him to arrange to pick up my tape and to inquire further about his interest or referrals.

2. PRESENT TO HUSBAND AND WIFE TOGETHER.

Do not delude yourself into thinking that you can present your program to one spouse without the other one being present and still succeed. Your prospect will never be able to explain the program to his or her spouse as compellingly as you can.

> **The First Five Points**
>
> 1. Qualify the appointment.
> 2. Show the plan to both husband and wife.
> 3. Prepare your performance.
> 4. Arrive early and stay late.
> 5. State how long you expect the meeting to last.

Save yourself a lot of time and grief by insisting that both parties be present when you arrive. If your prospect tells you that the husband/wife/significant other will not be there, and that they can make decisions for both, you say this:

"I can appreciate that. However, my boss (upline sponsor, supervisor, etc.) requires that I speak to the husband and wife together. When would be a good time to catch both of you together?"

If they refuse to let you present to both of them together, disqualify them. Believe me, you will not be losing a darn thing.

Luckily, I used this same approach with Joe and his wife, Mary. It took some effort to determine a schedule that would work for all three of us, but once we sat down together, I immediately realized the importance of following this step. By insisting that Mary attend the meeting, I was able to not only save myself the time of a repeat performance, but could also speak to Mary's desires as well as Joe's. I could double the selling power of my presentation.

3. PREPARE YOUR "BROADWAY" SALES PERFORMANCE.

I believe in having my presentation down cold before going on a sales call. I don't like winging something that can make me look foolish. The sales presentation deserves some serious attention if you're going to get it down pat. After all, didn't Yul Brynner deliver the exact same presentation more than 5,000 times in the Broadway play *The King and I*?

At the very least, I want to have the outline of my presentation in my head, so I know where I'm going (step by step) with my sales performance. It's a good idea to have the sequence of your presentation and your best-selling questions (written on three-by-five cards) with you. Refer to these cards (your prospects will not laugh at you) during your presentation to guarantee that you will stay on the right track. Do this until you know your presentation backward and forward. You won't be sorry.

When I met with Joe and Mary, I brought my three-by-five cards with me. Thank goodness I did! Mary later told me that she was really having doubts about being able to give a professional business presentation until she watched me with the cards. "I realized that if you could use the cards to present this plan, so could I," Mary told me. It was the single most important thing I did to help Mary see herself in this business.

Another good idea is to role-play as your prospect while you drive to your appointment. See yourself fielding questions and then transitioning to the next step.

Because I had already spoken with Joe on several occasions, I knew a few of his concerns and desires. I knew that he was very busy at the dry cleaners, working more than 60 hours a week. I also knew that Mary was a stay-at-home mom and had not ever worked outside of the home. By addressing this time concern up front and using the cards to show Mary that she could in fact help Joe in this business, I cinched the deal.

Powerful stuff, huh?

4. ARRIVE EARLY AND STAY LATE.

There are several benefits to arriving five to 10 minutes early for an appointment:

- You increase the chances that you will not be late (a real no-no).
- You will most likely get to spend some casual time "warming up" with your prospects before the serious discussions begin.

- You will convey to your prospects that you are responsible and punctual.

If your prospects are not ready to see you before the scheduled time, that's okay too. You can spend the time looking about, getting a feel for what your prospects are like before you actually meet them.

When you finish your sales performance, don't be in a hurry to leave. You can solidify your sale by developing the relationship even further. Often, you will discover other opportunities you didn't see before.

My appointment with Joe and Mary was scheduled for 7:00 P.M. I showed up 10 minutes early, just as Mary was making final arrangements for her two kids to go to a friend's house during our meeting. I was able to meet the kids and begin to develop a relationship with the family. In fact, after our meeting, Mary invited me to walk down to the neighbor's house to pick up her kids. It turned out to be a great opportunity, because her older daughter told Mary after the meeting that she would like to help her with the business—because she liked me!

Arriving early and staying late will also allow you to pace yourself better between appointments.

5. ADDRESS THE TIME ISSUE.

After you have greeted your prospects, ask them to give you an idea of how much time they have reserved for this meeting. Their response will tell you a great deal. You get to size up the situation by the amount of time they agree to give you. If their situation has changed and they cannot give you the time you need, you can reschedule the appointment to a time when you will not be rushed.

Asking your prospects about the time also conveys that you respect their time and do not plan to waste it, which they will appreciate.

With Joe and Mary, I knew how little time Joe spent at home with the family, and when I inquired as to the amount of time they had available, I wasn't surprised when they told me an hour. I didn't simply take the extra time for my full presentation, leaving them tapping their feet and glancing at their watches. They invited me to spend a couple of extra minutes with them.

6. GET THEM TO THE DINING TABLE.

The dining or kitchen table is a friendly place. It's where family and friends meet to "break bread." It's also often where family matters are discussed and important decisions are made. You need to get your prospects to the dining or kitchen table and position them exactly where you want them to sit. Here are a couple of things to say to make that happen:

"Mr. and Ms. Jones, could we go over to the dining table. I have some things to show you, and that way you might be able to see them a little better."

To position them to sit together, say this:

"Tell you what, you two sit together on this side of the table and I'll sit on this side. This way I can show this program to both of you at the same time." (They always comply.)

Joe and Mary spent so little time at the dining table that when I suggested we sit there, they almost seemed surprised. However, the room was so warm and cozy, and as we sat together around their table, we were able to continue to build upon the good relationships I had started earlier.

7. ELIMINATE ALL DISTRACTIONS.

Have you ever been a guest in a home where the constant noise made it difficult to think? Imagine how hard it is for the occupants themselves to have a clear thought! A television playing, children making noise, or dogs barking can kill the best of presentations. You never want to begin your sales performance in any of these situations.

> **The Next Five Points**
>
> 6. Position them at the table.
> 7. Eliminate all distractions.
> 8. Handle the "experts."
> 9. Set the stage for commitments.
> 10. Have your prospect "present" to you!

Here is the best language I've ever used to get the television to be turned off:

"Folks [point to the TV], I cannot compete with a professional. Would it be okay if I turn your TV down just a little so you can hear me better?" (They always jump up and turn it all the way off.)

If their children start climbing all over you, be courteous and smile, but completely stop talking. This will convey that you cannot continue with this kind of distraction.

If you have other distractions, such as dogs barking or children playing too loud, make this request:

"Folks, what we have to talk about tonight is extremely important. It's critical that I have your undivided attention. Is there any way we could put the dog and children into another room or something?" (They do.)

8. HANDLE THE "EXPERTS."

I cringe when I go to an appointment and discover that people are there that I hadn't counted on: like nosy neighbors, know-it-all friends, and family members that give unsolicited advice.

Unless you take drastic measures in these situations, you can be sure that when you finish your presentation, these people will play "expert" and advise your prospects to say no, think it over, or that they know of "a better deal somewhere else." Ugh!

In these cases, reschedule if at all possible. If that's not practical, go to Plan B. Bring everybody into the performance and sell them on it as a group.

Ask these folks if they would like to see the program too. (They always say yes.) Then, get everybody together at the dining table. As you ask your questions and create a state of agreement with your real prospects, do the same thing with the additional guests.

When you finish your "performance," if your real prospects are sold, generally so is everyone else. By having everybody participate and respond positively to your questions, chances are that you won't have a problem with these guests after you leave.

Occasionally, you'll get lucky and make multiple sign-ups!

When Mary invited me to walk with her to the neighbor's house, I was a bit concerned that the neighbor might start with the "20 questions." However, before we approached the door, I mentioned to Mary that I had another appointment soon after this one. This is one way I was able to sidestep trying to give her neighbor a presentation as we stood in the doorway.

By the way, if someone comes over to visit with your prospects in the middle of your presentation (thereby interrupting your performance), what do you do? You stop talking until they leave or you invite them into the action and bring them up to date with what you've covered so far.

9. SET THE STAGE FOR COMMITMENTS.

One of the most important aspects of giving a successful presentation is to set the stage for what you want your prospects to do during your performance. I don't know about you, but I want my prospects saying "yes" to my questions and responding positively to everything I show them as I move along.

Here is what I say to easily get a "yes" response for each step of my demonstration:

"Mr. and Ms. Smith, the last thing in the world I would want to do is get you folks involved in a business that you do not feel comfortable with. Please stop me if you're concerned about any part of my presentation. By the same token, as we discuss the program, I'll be asking you some questions to get your feedback. If I feel there is not a good fit, I'll suggest that we discontinue the demonstration and we can still part friends. Would that be okay with you?"

When I met with Joe and Mary, I mentioned that I knew in advance some of the likely objections or concerns that would come up. I hit those concerns head on by saying, "Listen Joe, I know you are already just about maxed out at work and that the last thing in the world you probably need is more time away from your family." Boy, I sure got his attention, and both he and Mary nodded their heads in agreement. "What I am going to share with you tonight will take some time, but together I think we can outline a plan that will work for the two of you and will take into consideration your time constraints," I added. I could see Joe and Mary relax, and am confident they listened more attentively than they might have otherwise.

This staging of the presentation for commitment enhances the responses given by your prospects. The reason for this: You are letting your prospects know in advance that they have to meet your program's qualifications just as your program must meet their requirements.

10. HAVE YOUR PROSPECT PRESENT TO YOU.

Sounds crazy, doesn't it? But that's exactly what will happen when you open your sales dialogue with a question that reveals their hot buttons. Questions like this:

- "Would you give me your thoughts about the discussion we had earlier on the phone?"
- "What was it about this program that attracted your attention?"
- "Why did you folks decide to invite me here this evening to see this program?"

Follow up with problem, probing, and benefit questions around the answers they give you, and you will have *them* doing most of the talking (and selling) for you. You can then customize your talk (and questions) around what's important to them.

Joe told me that after our first conversation at the dry cleaners, he spent a lot of time thinking about the path that he was on and the many hours of family time he was missing. He began to wonder, "Is there a way out for me? Is it possible that I could develop an income on the side that might free me from these many hours away from Mary and the kids? What if this could work for me?"

So when I asked Joe to give me his thoughts after listening to the tape, he was loaded with information! He began to sell me (and Mary) on his dreams and goals. The more he talked, the more excited he became. And you should have seen Mary. She kept leaning closer and closer to the table and, eventually, reached out and took Joe's hand while he continued to tell us why this business would be the answer to many of his dreams.

Once he got Mary going, she began to open up as well, sharing some of her personal feelings and thoughts about her life. It was an incredible time, one that I had prepared for by doing my homework and inviting Joe to get involved in my presentation.

Rehearsal Time!

Let's quickly review those 10 points we've just learned (because we need to begin practicing them right away!).

1. Qualify the appointment.
2. Present only to husband and wife together.
3. Prepare your "Broadway" sales performance.
4. Arrive early and stay late.
5. Address the time issue.
6. Get them to the dining table.
7. Eliminate all distractions.
8. Handle the "experts."
9. Set the stage for commitments.
10. Have your prospects present to you.

Only by preparing for a "golden opportunity" will you ever get one. Great performances don't happen overnight; they happen with time. Constant practice, preparation, and continual performance will ultimately allow you to become as comfortable with presenting the Quixtar opportunity as you are having a casual conversation with your spouse.

There you have it—the formula for success in building your downline. Follow these simple steps to success closely; polish your skills for prospecting and showing the plan, and your business organization may grow to hundreds of thousands!

P A R T   T H R E E

Do It!

CHAPTER TEN

Motivational Mastery

You've dreamed it, you've dared it, and now you've come to the part of the book where you have to do it! All of the dreaming, all of the daring and planning, will come to nothing if you don't take those first scary steps and get out there and DO IT.

What have you accomplished so far? Pat yourself on the back; you have done a great deal making your way through the previous chapters. You are well on your way to building up your income, to taking advantage of your chance to truly create wealth on the Web!

I've given you an inside look at how to find prospects to build your business, and how to then sit down and talk to them about becoming Quixtar IBOs. But once you get them to sign up, uh, then what happens? Do they just march out into the streets and become successful? Alas, no. You might upon occasion find someone to add to your organization that can just march out and do it on his own, but you will find that with most folks, you will need to help them achieve. You will need to motivate those miners, those folks who are joining with you in the quest to strike gold on the Net.

This is where the rubber meets the road in building a business of any kind, and it is critical to your success as an IBO. In the months and years ahead, you'll find yourself returning to this chapter again and again. Because even the best and most successful Quixtar IBOs have learned that a motivational shot in the arm is needed frequently!

High-Tech/High-Touch

One of the true aces that Quixtar holds in the Internet world is that it is both a high-tech and high-touch business. It is not just a faceless e-commerce Web site but rather one that is backed by individuals that you know and with whom you interact. It is a large network of folks who are committed to each other's success. Quixtar just happens to be the ideal vehicle for them to get there. What do I mean by high-tech, high-touch? I mean that you will be highly involved in touching the lives of the people in your high-tech organization by helping them succeed and build up their own organizations. You will help to keep them motivated, pumped up about the future that is within their reach.

Why are some people successful while others are not? Why do some people risk while others don't? In many cases, it is due to the results of self-limiting beliefs. Have you ever looked at a person in your downline and thought, "Gee, they have it all. They are going to go straight to the top," only to find out months or years later that although they *seemed* to have it all, there were things that just kept coming up and getting in the way of accomplishment? Some may have been real obstacles, some self-imposed. It happens all the time. We collect self-limiting beliefs in all areas of our life: love, pain, fear, image, communication, money, responsibility, expectations, emotional, physical, spiritual, intellectual, professional, and social.

Self-Limiting Beliefs?

You may ask: How do I know if I have these beliefs? How do I know which of the people in my downline have these beliefs and what can

I do about it? First, let's take a look at how these beliefs manifest themselves:

I'm not: good enough, lovable, intelligent, responsible, as good as so-and-so, wanted, pretty, thin, handsome, worthy, fun, happy, content, confident, cared for, loved for who I am, creative, perfect, emotional, talkative, adequate, masculine, feminine, sexy.

I am too: intense, fat, thin, tall, short, stupid, aggressive, closed, shy, weird, scattered, selfish, unattractive, lazy, immature, mature, serious, sensitive, depressed, crazy, different, spoiled, intelligent, understanding, trusting.

I fear: honesty, success, sickness, poverty, criticism, rejection, loneliness, appearing weak, getting angry, being vulnerable, being wrong, being out of control, being a loser, being left out, feeling judged, being abandoned, being controlled, knowing myself, loss of love, knowing others' true feelings, being a failure, being unmasculine, being unfeminine, being boring, being closed, being unacceptable, getting old, feeling stupid, feeling unworthy, being inadequate, being incompetent, appearing foolish.

So, do any of these characteristics sound familiar to you? All too many of us frequently hear these kinds of thoughts in our heads. If we aren't beating ourselves up about our thighs or our "abs," then we are fretting about what our friends and loved ones think of us.

Where *Does* This Come From?

In our center—at the very top of the stomach—is where beliefs start. You can feel it right there when someone says something hurtful or if you suddenly become afraid. Depending on what we hear or feel about ourselves, we create beliefs that begin to limit us. If you live with these beliefs long enough, and believe they are true on an emotional level, you have created a self-limiting emotion, which is even *stronger* than any belief. Once you start making choices based on these beliefs and emotions, they produce self-limiting behaviors.

How does that affect your business? In so many ways: fear of approaching someone, fear of rejection, prejudging a situation, fearing success or failure. These fears keep us from taking action, and inaction is a self-limiting behavior. These beliefs stop us before we ever get started and drain us of our energy.

Our job is to build relationships and motivate people who believe they can and will become successful at their Internet business. Our job is to encourage them and inspire them.

If we buy into the limited beliefs that they have about themselves, then their business, and in turn our growth, is doomed. But if we help them grow beyond those limited beliefs, we help free them to succeed.

We need to continually give our people the pats on the back they need, the complements and the praise, to keep them motivated and striving for the next level of success.

Many successful IBOs have said, in looking back, that their biggest regret is having spent too much time with the wrong people. I absolutely believe this. However, I have been in this business for almost 20 years, and I still sometimes find it difficult to tell the right people from the wrong people at the outset.

I can think of countless examples of prospects and business builders that I thought were going to be superstars, but didn't turn out to be. Thankfully, I can think of far more who, with the proper motivation, did turn out to be superstars.

What do I look for? Who do I think I can motivate? I look for people who do what they say they will do. For people who, day in and day out, get things accomplished in their lives—*not* a guy who sits around on the couch in front of the TV recounting his past glory days as a high school football hero, *not* a woman who complains all day long on the phone to her friends about how unhappy she is in her marriage.

I'm looking for the guy who gets up early every morning to swim laps at the gym, or the woman who steps in to organize the kids' car ool and creates a phone tree to keep other mothers informed of the changes. You know, people who get stuff done!

Executive Diamond Jim Floor shared this idea with me: "Motivation comes from commitment. First it starts with a decision, for example, the decision to build this business. But when that decision moves from your head, from thinking, into your heart, an emotion, it becomes commitment. It becomes a hunger for things that will propel you toward your goal."

When first starting off as an IBO, almost everybody is excited. They are filled with big dreams and big aspirations, but not everyone can keep going, day in and day out. What it takes to keep going every day is what Jim Floor described as, "the hunger, and the commitment that will propel you toward your goal."

As a leader, the words I like to hear most from an IBO are: "Okay, Cynthia, what shall I do next?"

Anyone who is coming back to me asking for more advice, for more guidance, for more motivation, is coming back because they have completed something already and are looking to do more. "I listened to that tape you gave me, it was great! Do you have any more like it?" "I've already called my top 25 names, who do you think I should call next?" These are folks who are willing to learn.

Leadership Ability

Are the right people self-motivated, self-reliant visionaries? If they are, then they are few and far between. Don't get discouraged. You are looking for people with leadership ability who are willing to do the work that is necessary to get them where they say they want to go. If they are not willing to do the work, they are the wrong people. It is that simple. Let go and move on.

Can leaders be developed? Yes! But only if they want to be. Sometimes, people don't realize that they have the desire or capacity to be a leader until it is pointed out to them. Sometimes that means having them take a personal inventory. Learn to ask some soul-searching questions:

Where do you see yourself in five years?
What really matters to you?
If you could live your life any way you want to, what would you be doing now?
What do you feel is stopping you from living your dream?
What are your greatest strengths and what is your greatest weakness?
What do you fear most?

Jim Floor says, "I don't believe I can motive anyone. It has to come from inside them." That is why it is very important to get your new IBOs trained and working according to your company's system right away. Watch them; coach them when they need it. When people keep making excuses, send them tapes and books on personal effectiveness training and let them go.

They have to decide what they want. If they really want to move in the direction of personal achievement and fulfillment, they will take responsibility for themselves, and you may find that you have your leader. You will have provided a service for that person that they will never forget. If you don't make these distinctions between leadership candidates, you may be spending too much time with the wrong people. Your time and energy is valuable. Don't waste it trying to fix others or questioning your ability.

However, when you do discover a leader, imagine how great the feeling! Jim Floor describes it like this: "Our lifestyle is terrific today, but more important than the financial reward, more important than freedom or even the friendships, is the discovery of the potential that lies within myself and that I now see in others. Helping them with their own discovery is the greatest reward I have."

What Held Me Back

I am grateful that the person who first introduced me to this industry didn't buy into my own self-limiting beliefs. I broke free with a nudge in the right direction. Let me tell you about my first stumbling steps . . .

I was living in a small town in Northern California, in a very pleasant neighborhood, when a soon-to-be doctor of veterinary medicine and his wife bought a beautiful Victorian down the street. I was intrigued by their lifestyle—how could a young couple afford such a big house? And they were always so happy and upbeat, what *was* their secret?

One day I asked, and they told me their secret—network marketing. "Yuck!" I thought to myself, "I could *never* do that! Talk to strangers? No way!" The idea of approaching strangers was frightening.

The couple gently pointed out that I did in fact speak to strangers already, all day long on the RV lot my husband and I owned. "But those people come to me, I don't go out seeking them. They come there because they want what I have. It's different!"

Where did my motivation come from? How did I conquer my fear? With the help and encouragement of my sponsors, the vet student and his wife, I stopped focusing on myself and my fears and started focusing on all the benefits I would be offering. Why hesitate to speak to strangers if I believed that what I had to offer could make a real difference in their lives?

Become the Person You Want To Be

When I went to my first business meeting, I was inspired, excited, and I was challenged. I knew that in order to achieve in this industry, I would have to become the person I always knew I could be but was afraid to become. One step at a time made it less overwhelming. Instead of being afraid, I got excited. This business has done more than give me a healthy income. It gave me my life back. I became someone I felt proud to be. I had plenty of self-limiting beliefs that were not supporting my success. In order to gain success, I had to modify my self-limiting beliefs and focus on what was constructive. Of course, the journey isn't over yet, not by a long shot. Today I am still evolving and growing.

I'd like to recommend a course of action. First, ask yourself the following questions pertaining to your business and use the information you get to find the talents and qualities within you, which are your own personal ingredients for success:

How are you playing the game of Internet business—full out or sitting in the stands?
What choices are you making and why?
What is your self-talk? Are you speaking the language of success?
What feelings are you experiencing on this journey? Fear? Excitement?
What is limiting the way you are playing?
How and when are you holding back?
How is this a mirror for other choices you make in life?

We must consciously choose the beliefs that will help us in our desire to get to the top of our game. Here a few examples of "limiting beliefs" versus "positive beliefs":

Limiting—Quixtar is saturated because so many people are already doing it!

Positive—I love this business. It is growing so fast. I no longer have to convince people about how great it is. It is obvious because of all the people who are getting involved.

Limiting—I don't know if I can handle all of the changes going on in my life. There are so many obstacles to overcome. I feel overwhelmed.

Positive—I am constantly being prepared to handle every situation. I am grateful for all the opportunities in my life.

There will always be limiting beliefs in our lives, but we increase our opportunity for success by concentrating on beliefs that lend 100 percent support to the conviction that success is possible.

Second, create a statement of purpose, which you can repeat out loud throughout the day. Make sure it speaks to who you are. Ask yourself these questions and form your statement from their answers:

- Why do I do what I do?
- Does my purpose communicate who I am?
- Does my purpose inspire me?
- Who am I emotionally?
- What makes me unique?
- What do I value?
- What do I believe about myself?
- Who do I want to be when I grow up?

Imagine this: We can have awesome success the same way we have limited success! Do what the successful people do in your upline—listen to tapes, go to seminars, and find a coach or a mentor. Concentrate first on growing as a person, and your bank account will start growing in step with your personal growth. Some of my favorite words for helping me stay on track are: intention, purpose, vision, action, accountability, authenticity, and commitment. Maybe these are some of your favorite words too. To keep myself in a positive frame of mind, I have this phrase framed in my office: "God is Watching, Give Him a Good Show!"

What Is Your Dream?

When I started my business career, no one asked me if I had experience; rather, they asked me if I had a dream. I love this industry, and I am very grateful for the life I have been able to create because of it. Today my purpose is to create an environment of challenge, enlightenment, and progression for anyone who is on that type of journey. This is done through loving, open, and honest communication and with a deep level of compassion and understanding. My greatest tools are my faith, courage, and determination. I have seen the past. My interest is only in today, to do the very best I can, and in the future for who I can become.

The Best Motivation of All

There is only one sure-fire way to motivate your people—be the best you can be and lead by example. You can teach, inspire, and offer support and information, but your people will determine the end result themselves. How big is their dream, their *why*? What is the level of their commitment? How willing are they to learn and to listen? Are they teachable? Success is an inside job—it develops within the person you're motivating.

The bottom line is that we can best motivate others by example. And in order to do that effectively, we must concentrate on motivating ourselves! Don't make the mistake of giving so much to your team that you leave yourself drained and exhausted from the effort. Keep plenty of time set aside so that *you* too can listen to the motivational tapes, so that you can spend a quiet 20 minutes at night getting jazzed by reading a motivational book. Every minute you invest in motivating yourself, in staying upbeat and positive in the face of an uphill climb, will manifest itself many times over in the people who make up your organization.

CHAPTER ELEVEN

Go for It!

You've now read through 10 chapters designed to give you the information you need to succeed as a Quixtar IBO—everything from what is happening in the fast-paced world of e-commerce and how Quixtar fits in, to how to build your own business as an IBO and attract forward-thinking entrepreneurs to build their independent businesses with you.

But the biggest question is . . . whether you will take advantage of this once in a lifetime opportunity? Will you go for it and start building your financial future today using this phenomenal business opportunity?

How Many Times Does a Great Opportunity Come Knocking?

So many of us have said this before: "If only I'd invested in that stock years ago, it would be worth a fortune now!" Or this: "If only I'd bought a house in that neighborhood 20 years ago, it would be worth a million dollars now!" Or even this: "If only I'd taken a chance on buying one of those hamburger franchises in the '60s, I'd be sitting on easy street today."

But you didn't buy the stock, the house, or the hamburger franchise. Why not? Was the opportunity available to you? It probably was if you'd wanted it badly enough. The folks who did go ahead and buy the stock, the house, or the franchise all had to take the plunge and do something that wasn't necessarily going to be a sure thing. The folks who did go ahead had to listen to their neighbors, family, and friends scoff at their foolishness, sometimes even being told, "It will never work. This is the dumbest idea I've ever heard of! You can't do it." But these brave people tuned out these negative messages, and years later their bravery, foresight, and courage was rewarded many times over.

For of all sad words of tongue or pen,
The saddest are these: "It might have been!"
—John Greenleaf Whittier

You have that same opportunity to be rewarded as a Quixtar IBO. If you commit yourself to taking advantage of this opportunity today and devote the next few years to building it up as big as you can, who knows how large your fortunes could be? Like taking the chance early on a stock, a piece of real estate, or a small business, the return could well be a thousandfold. It is up to you. Dexter Yager told me that the money he has made in the past (remember $5 million in just one year) will look like peanuts compared to the income IBOs will create with Quixtar! Is it going to be big? You better believe it!

Is this yet another golden opportunity that will pass you by, yet another lost opportunity that years from now you will look back on and say, "If only I'd given that Quixtar business a chance, I'd be worth a fortune now!"

"Sometimes I can't sleep at night thinking about the potential of my business," Kevin Wilson told me. "The opportunities are endless. I'm a Navy pilot, and I love what I do, but this really made sense.

Growing my business is an opportunity that I'm not going to miss out on." Kevin has been a Quixtar IBO since it launched in September 1999, and he believes he is on his way to achieving his goal of financial freedom.

Consider This!

How many times does opportunity knock on your door? Sometimes only once!

"Quixtar is 12 to 24 months ahead of the game," Jim Floor told me as we sat in his beautiful, spacious office. "This business is primed to explode in the next couple of years. Similar to the auto industry after the completion of roads, so will be our business explosion as we continually increase our user-friendly product and add more and more partner stores. We are running at Internet speed now! People with the vision will be postured for exponential growth."

Don't let this one slip by! Don't miss your opportunity to get in now, in the early years, and prosper along with this burgeoning technology.

Catch the Wave of E-Commerce

Remember what we talked about in Chapter Four, E-Commerce Explodes? Do you think that the huge interest in the Internet will go away soon? Will it just disappear overnight like a shady circus set up on the edge of town? Take it from me—it's not likely to happen. Instead, what I (and thousands of technology experts) believe will happen is this: Much of everyday life and everyday living will have some kind of Internet focus to it. Whether it is how we coordinate our children's after-school soccer schedules or how we get our cars serviced, things that we can't imagine doing with a computer now will become absolutely routine.

> **Imagine the Future**
>
> Technology experts believe that the Internet and e-commerce will grow into something so large, the likes of which we have never seen before! Stake your claim today!

As I write this chapter in the summer of 2000, two large online grocery home delivery companies just announced that they will merge. Is this because they think the market is getting smaller? Uh, no, they don't think the market is getting smaller. Webvan and HomeGrocer think the market for these kinds of services is growing by leaps and bounds. Why do I mention this particular business development? Because home delivery of your basic staples is one of the core products of Quixtar!

As a matter of fact, Quixtar business giant Jody Victor told me the very same day that this Webvan news broke that "We are in the replenishment business." What does he mean by that? That with Quixtar's Ditto Delivery system, deliveries of basic commodities to buyers' homes are available on a regularly scheduled basis. And that, folks, is an important element in building your business! The more IBOs and members there are in your organization who choose to use this great service, the greater the financial rewards for everyone.

Two IBOs who couldn't be more excited about the prospects for e-commerce are Lou and Barbara De Luca. He's a retired professional hockey player, and she is a former champion figure skater and now coach. "We are unique in what we offer on the Web as Quixtar IBOs," they told me. "Now, word of mouth *really* works to build the business!"

Brand New Industries Become the Basis of Big Fortunes

A few chapters ago I talked about some of the old family fortunes, the families with famous names like Rockefeller and Carnegie.

How did the founders of these fortunes manage to grow their businesses so large—large enough that the money has gone on for many generations?

Did men like John D. Rockefeller and Andrew Carnegie get involved in a proven industry that had been around for decades? No. Did they enter into fields where the path to success was well established and certain? No. For the most part, these were brand-new, emerging industries that were far from certain successes, but these visionary men could see what the future held for them. Rockefeller envisioned a future where the car was king, where the automobile industry would grow, and he saw that all of those cars would need gasoline. Carnegie saw a future in which buildings would require steel frame construction instead of wood and masonry.

Was the Sears fortune founded on a proven idea? If you sent out a catalog filled with merchandise to folks who lived away from a store, would those same folks order products from you to be sent through the mail? Trust me, it was a kooky idea at the time! Did the businessmen who took chances to build railroads nationwide have any idea that financial success was certain? No, but they laid that track down anyway. Quixtar is your chance to do the same thing, to leap into the unknown and bravely build your own future. Don't miss your best chance to get involved in the infancy of an industry—e-commerce—and ride it all the way to the top!

A Brave New World

Quixtar is your chance to leap into the unknown and bravely build your future yourself! Don't miss your best chance to get involved in the infancy of an industry—e-commerce—and ride it all the way to the top!

You Don't Have to Go It Alone!

Some of the risk-taking business pioneers I've just been talking about were solo acts; they built up their companies on their own.

But you have an even better opportunity: to be in the vanguard with your family and friends!

I'll admit it, starting any kind of business is a risk. You risk your money, your time, and your efforts. But as a Quixtar-affiliated IBO, you can lessen the risk of loneliness, which is one of the biggest things entrepreneurs complain about! Instead of working long hours alone in an emerging field, you can invest those hours in happily helping your friends, family, and neighbors succeed along with you. And they will help you, in turn.

I say, why be lonely at the top when you can make sure the people you care about get there at the same time you do? Many of the top income earners in Quixtar told me that the greatest joy they know is to work side by side with their children, developing a family business that not only pays well but also lasts several lifetimes.

Don't overlook the benefits of belonging to this extraordinary Quixtar community. The benefits are not all just financial, either, but emotional as well. Speaking from my own experience, I've seen time and time again how IBOs are brought together outside of the world of business in order to celebrate life's triumphs and overcome life's tragedies.

Jody Victor told me about someone in his organization who recently suffered a seizure and was hospitalized. The hospital staff was astonished at the number of inquiries and mail they received for this patient. Was she a celebrity, they wondered? No, she was an ordinary woman who was involved in an extraordinary business. Because she had met thousands of people over the years at business training seminars and other functions, these same people took a special interest in her. "She is a part of our community," Jody said. "Once the word got out on her condition, people on three different continents were offering prayers on her behalf."

I too have made remarkably strong friendships through this business. Although my primary reason for getting involved was financial, I have been repeatedly blessed by the relationships with those folks that I have worked with night after night.

Becoming involved with Quixtar can literally change your whole life. Strong friendships, the relationship you have with your family, and the way you view yourself and what you are capable of—the benefits are endless.

Do *You* Have What It Takes?

What does it really take to be the kind of person who decides to take a risk and build a railroad, buy an unknown stock, or build a house in a new neighborhood? What does it take to be the kind of person whose forward-thinking courage is rewarded financially? What does it take to be a successful Quixtar IBO?

Industry giants like Dexter Yager say, "It starts with a dream." Without the *why*, the *what* doesn't matter. In Chapter Two, I encouraged you to think big and define your dream. Without defining that dream, without deciding what it is that motivates you to succeed, all of your hard work will be squandered. It takes a *dream*.

What else does it take to succeed as a Quixtar IBO? Let's take a look at a brief list:

- Motivation and enthusiasm
- The desire for more out of life
- The willingness to learn from others who have succeeded
- The willingness to help others succeed
- Focus and follow-through

MOTIVATION AND ENTHUSIASM

Enthusiasm is contagious. It is not simply words but rather an energy that envelops you and helps you see what is possible. It gives you the hope and belief that your dreams are possible for you too. You need to surround yourself with motivated and enthusiastic people. This is a role that your upline fills for you and that you will need to fill for the IBOs that you register.

THE DESIRE FOR MORE OUT OF LIFE

The desire and drive to build your business as an IBO starts with the desire to do something more with your life. Whether the "more" is getting braces for your young teenage daughter or securing private golf lessons for yourself, the motivation comes from within. Building a Quixtar-affiliated IBO business won't always be easy. You need a solid desire, the "dream" that Dexter Yager talks about, in order to keep going day after day, meeting after meeting.

Kentucky-based radio celebrity Jack Fox and his wife, Lou, are building their Quixtar-affiliated business. Jack has spent years in the radio business, and his wife has worked for years as a nurse, but it was always on someone else's payroll. As Jack told me recently, "We are working hard to build up this business, but here we get paid for our performance!" Jack and Lou are well on their way to getting much more out of life than just a paycheck.

THE WILLINGNESS TO LEARN FROM OTHERS WHO HAVE SUCCEEDED

Are you willing to listen? Are you willing to set your ego down on the chair next to you and listen willingly to someone else—to ask for advice and then, even more importantly, to put that advice into action? Many IBOs have experienced career and business success in other fields before entering the Internet arena. You already know a thing or two, of course you do. But the folks who succeed quickly here are the folks who recognize that they can benefit from the experience of others.

THE WILLINGNESS TO HELP OTHERS SUCCEED

Much of your success is tied to the success of those you bring into this business with you—the faster they grow and become financially successful, the better off you are financially.

Who succeeds in this business? The people who take real delight and joy in helping others build their businesses. They succeed not just because they see dollar signs, but also because they enjoy being a part of someone else's achievements. Imagine the rewards you'll feel when someone in your organization reaches her financial goal and is now able to stay home and raise her children. Imagine the rewards you'll feel when you watch as someone you've been working with is able to cut back on his hours and pursue his lifelong dream of writing a book. Does this sound like you?

Lou and Barbara De Luca shared a story about a new IBO who joined their organization: "He's a great guy, but his people skills aren't hot. He's socially awkward. Yet, by being able to drive people to his Web site to learn more—instead of having to talk a lot—he is doing fine. His business is growing. We are thrilled for him." With Lou and Barbara's help, he is well on his way!

FOCUS AND FOLLOW-THROUGH

It's easy to become distracted or sidetracked in life; it happens to all of us. But when trying to build a business as a Quixtar IBO, this can be not only costly in your business but also fatal. *Focus* is critical to your success and to the success of those IBOs you bring into business with you. Staying homed in on the fundamentals of success, or the eight steps to success I taught you in Chapters Six and Seven, will not only help you stay focused but also help you follow through on the goals and commitments you have set for yourself.

Am I describing you? I think I am!

Thinking Big Again!

I also believe that you are a big thinker. What makes me think that? If you didn't already have what it takes to succeed, you would never have bought this book. If you weren't a big thinker, you'd be home sitting on the recliner with the remote control in your hand, clicking through the commercials of fancy things that you would never be able to afford.

But that's not you. You are a person of courage. You are someone who is bold enough to seize an opportunity when the moment is right. And the moment is now.

Are you a big thinker? Yes, you are. You know that your dreams, your goals, and your desires can all be achieved through hard work and effort. You are strong enough to put aside your fears and press on through the hard times you will sometimes encounter as an Internet entrepreneur.

Are you afraid to grow rich? No. You know that you deserve wealth and success in your life. And you know that your dreams are possible and within your reach.

Act and Grow Rich!

We all know the old Napoleon Hill motivational book, *Think and Grow Rich*. Hill makes some wonderful points, but let's change that title around a bit. Of course, I want you to *think;* I want you to be thinking and planning all the time about how you can grow rich as a Quixtar IBO. But here is what I'd like you to adopt as your new mantra: *act and grow rich*. In order to succeed at anything, you must *act* upon your thoughts. You must recognize the opportunities that life presents you with, and you must have the courage to act upon them!

Don't Miss Your Chance!

Your opportunity to act and grow rich is now. There has never before been a time in history like this—a time when you have the opportunity to get involved and become financially successful in a new industry.

Here is what I believe: There will be many millionaires created as a result of their efforts in developing an online business with Quixtar. A crazy idea? I don't think so, and I've been given a very close look at the inner workings and what the future holds for this business. Visionary IBOs will seize the opportunity to build a business that will span the world for generations to come.

Will you be a part of it? *The choice is up to you.*

APPENDIX A

Take a Look at Quixtar

Now that you know exactly what to do to build your own e-commerce business, let's take a peek into the Quixtar site. The following pages will show you what the Quixtar site looks like, at least now, during the last quarter of 2000. Remember, Quixtar is constantly upgrading their site and adding new features and benefits for you, the Quixtar IBO.

Appendix A will walk you through the site, page by page, showing you some of the hottest features and benefits of the Quixtar site. You'll see how easy it is to go shopping (my personal favorite!), to manage your business, and to keep track of your growing and developing new company. So come on! What are we waiting for? Let's see what's happening at the hottest new address in cyberspace, Quixtar.

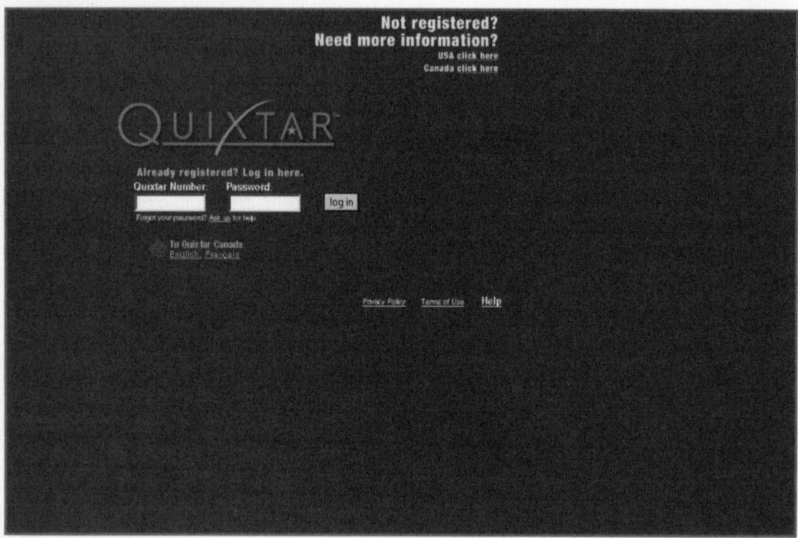

Log into Quixtar

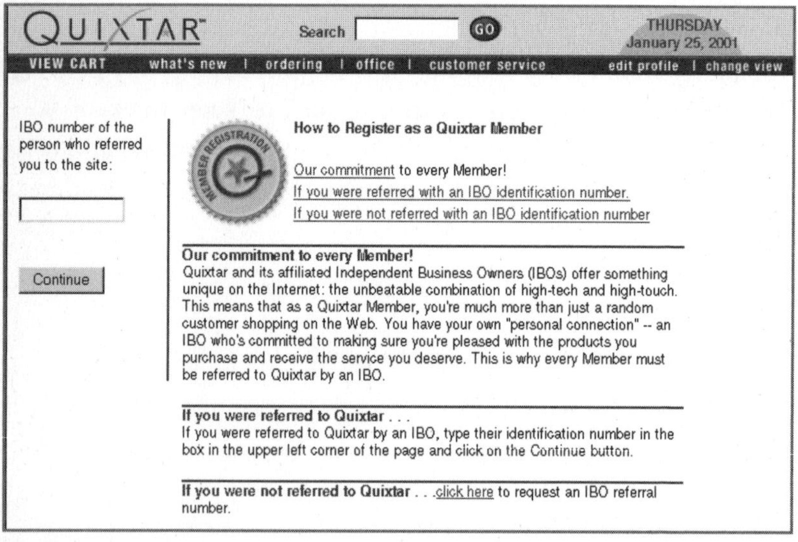

Register as a Quixtar Member

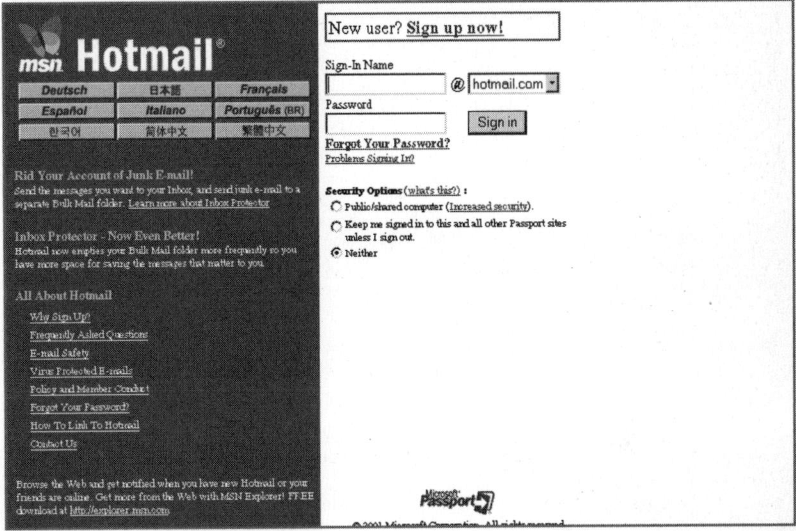

Set-up a Hotmail account

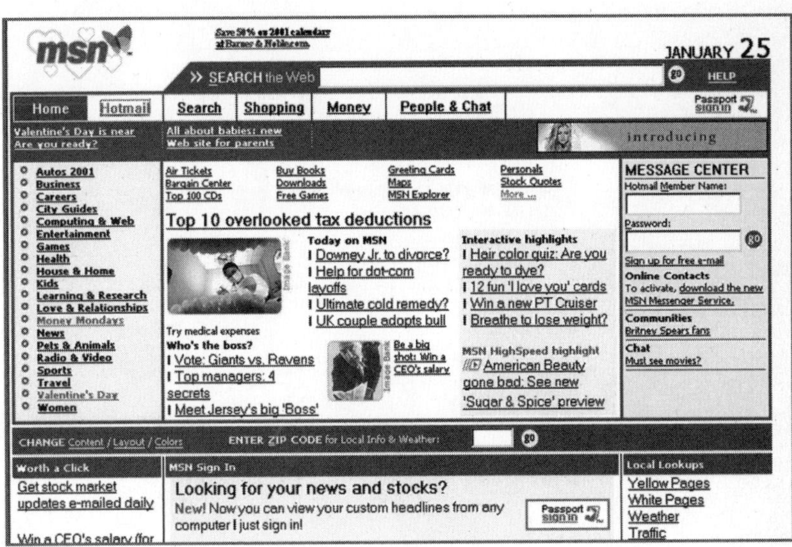

Check out all of the Hotmail options

Marketing Tips	My Organization		Auto Network	General		
Meeting Support	PV/BV		IBO Visa Card	Help		
	Business Information					
	Diamonds Only					

go shopping

<Top of page>

My Home	My Health	My Self	Hot Buys	Store for More	Partner Stores	Edit Profile
Laundry	Vitamins & Herbals	Hair Salon		Fashion	Quick List	Shopping
Cleaners & Disinfectants	Performance Foods	Skin Care		Health	How It Works	
Water Treatment	Therapeutic Magnets	Cosmetics Counter		Foods	Special Offers	General
Cookware & Cutlery	Weight Management	Aromatherapy		Home	What's New	Help
Tableware				Essentials	Rewards Brochure	
Crystal/Giftware				Seasonal		
Home Services				Get Catalog		
Special Features				PS Gift Service		
My Home	My Health	My Self				
Special Offers	Special Offers	Special Offers		Educational Programs		
Expert Advice/FAQ	Expert Advice/FAQ	Expert Advice/FAQ		SFM Home Page		
My Assessment	My Assessment	My Assessment		Hot Buys		

Find the right products

Explore the shopping home page

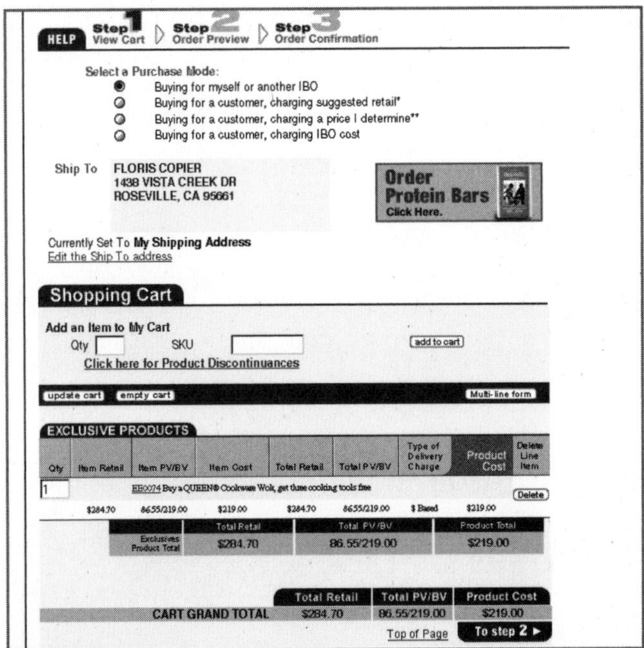

Follow the ordering process steps

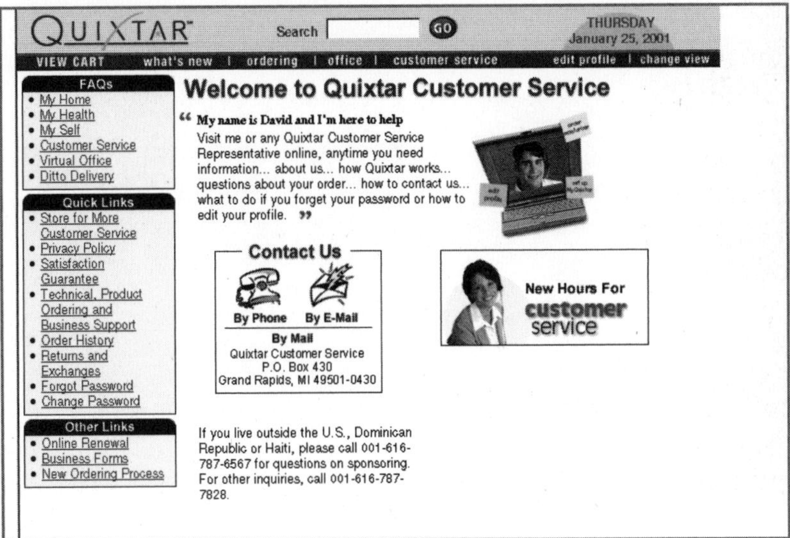

Take advantage of Quixtar's customer service

APPENDIX B

The Motivator's Manual

Congratulations on making the decision to build a Quixtar business! You are taking the first bold steps toward building your future and constructing your dream life. Years from now, you will look back and smile with pleasure at what you have accomplished since that first day.

In Appendix B, I've pulled together some extra tools to help those of you who are ready to get going right away to build organizations and downlines that will enable you to live the lifestyle of your dreams. Here is what you'll find in these powerful sections:

- **MLM and the Internet.** How have super achievers used the Internet to build their business organizations? Quixtar is a high-tech, high-touch organization, and in the following, I will tell you how to harness the high-tech aspect in order to benefit from the high-touch aspect.
- **12-Month Game Plan.** Once you take your first few steps, where are you headed? Here you'll find a solid, yearlong approach to building your business that will get you well on your way to success.

- **Five Tips for Telephone Invitations.** You reach for the phone, take a deep breath, dial the number, and then what? Use these handy scripts to help you navigate your way through your first telephone invitations. You'll soon get the hang of it.
- **Beyond Chicken and Egg.** Which should you show first—the product or the opportunity? Neither one, in fact; first you need to teach your prospects how to grow a business.

Dive right in and get going today! Time is "a-wasting," and someone else might be talking to your top prospects about Quixtar this very minute. Don't let another day go by without seizing this incredible opportunity.

Quixtar and the Internet

It seems the hot topic right now is "How can I use the Internet to build my Quixtar business?"

To help build my business, I have been using the Internet for two years now, and since September 1, 1999, I now have several people in my downline who use it almost exclusively. So let me share some of my opinions (stick with me on this one . . . *all* of the juicy details are provided).

First, the Internet should be viewed as just another lead generation source, rather than your only business-building technique. We are in the *leader building* business. No matter how you look at it, you can't create a leader out of somebody who is in his underwear in the spare bedroom, sitting behind his computer for eight hours a day hitting the "check e-mail" button every two minutes, hoping that the e-mail will come from someone who will build him a huge business.

Unfortunately, too many people get caught up in the Internet and this becomes their daily method of operation (I was there once too!). The problem is, this type of activity does not encourage personal growth, rather it actually hinders or even reverses personal growth. Pretty soon hours turn into days, days turn into weeks, weeks into months, and the next thing you know it is the year 2002 and the last book you've read was last month's *TV Guide!*

On the contrary, leaders are the ones going out and meeting new people, giving presentations on a regular basis, working with their people, and focusing on a strong local group that they will use as leverage for a national and international downline. They also spend time daily on their personal growth by reading books, going to seminars, and listening to tapes.

Am I suggesting you toss the computer out the window? No, not at all. The Internet can be a good, inexpensive way to generate new prospects, educate your current prospects on your company, and follow up with your older list of prospects. However, do not get so caught up in the Net that it becomes the *only* thing you do.

At any given time, you should have three to five methods of generating new, interested prospects; make the Internet *one* of those five techniques. I spend about one to two hours a day promoting my Web site, following up, and answering e-mails. I spend three to six hours a day doing things "off-line" and locally to build my business.

It has been my experience that it is much easier to build a business and work with your people when they are "in your own backyard." It is more difficult when they are scattered all across the country with no local support group.

However, I would have wasted my time and yours if I stopped here and did not share some practical, how-to advice and juicy tips on what works with the Internet and Quixtar.

Some Practical Pointers

Here are some powerful concepts you need to know to successfully use the Internet to help you build your online business:

ONE OF MANY WAYS

The Internet should be viewed as simply another lead generation source, *not* your only business-building technique. You need personal contact with your upline, downline, and prospects.

How do you generate leads? What we do is create a generic Web site. We offer visitors a reason to submit their e-mail addresses and to request information that says, "Yeah, I am looking for a home business, tell me what you've got for me." This is usually accomplished by offering a free report about starting a home business and having a catchy headline to get your visitor's attention.

(Oh, by the way, I forgot to say this: I *only* use the Net to generate potential business builders *not* product users. This is a personal choice based on my skills; both may be possible.)

FOLLOW UP!

Then, I endlessly follow up with these people via e-mail unless they (1) die, (2) change e-mail addresses, or (3) tell me they are not interested.

My follow-up looks like this:

First, they get a "presentation over e-mail." Each day I send my leads an e-mail. The first e-mail covers the industry, then our company, our products, our comp plan, why they should join me, about getting started, a follow-up about getting started, the tax advantages, and then I go into another follow-up sequence.

I also send out a message about once a month to everybody on my follow-up list. I use automated software for this. I have used and tested a lot of the software out there and have found that the more you automate the better. I spend about one hour a day online at this point, and I follow up with at least 50 people a day automatically. My entire online marketing system is self-operating. It *has* to be this way, otherwise people fall through the cracks and I would spend most of my day on tedious, nonproductive activities. "Automate or die" is my saying.

Everything I send these people is designed to educate them a little more, create a higher level of interest, and, most importantly, to get them to respond so we can start a conversation through e-mail and eventually over the phone. That is how you sponsor people—you create a dialog (build a relationship and trust) between the two of you.

You should figure that it will take anywhere from 50 to 100 prospects to sign up one new person using traditional online marketing techniques. To get somebody to move from a "cold lead" to a "prospect" to a new distributor can require anywhere from eight to 15 e-mails, each carrying different and useful information.

COLDER THAN COLD

The Internet is colder than your typical "cold market"; people can be down right nasty through e-mail due to the secrecy the Net provides. It also takes a lot longer to yield results than any other method out there. On average, a person will be on your follow-up list for a period ranging from one month to one year or more before they wish to join.

This is another reason why it is very important not to solely rely on the Internet. New people will give up far too early due to the slow results that come with this method of "cold calling." Don't get discouraged.

The Internet is very unduplicable. Yes, people with Internet experience and marketing can do what I do, and probably better, since I don't focus on it that much. But for newbies to join and think they can build a business completely online without knowing how to send e-mail or what a search engine is . . . you are talking about a two- to six-month-long education process just to understand the Internet . . . before they are at a point when they can consider using the Net to build a solid, long-term business.

SET THE EXAMPLE

People will be drawn by the way you sponsor them. I do not sponsor people over the Internet if their intention is to sit behind a computer screen in hopes of never talking to someone. I sponsor people who are willing to go out and build a good, sound business following my lead and training. The Internet might be one part of that bigger picture.

However, creating this bigger picture is hard to do. People are often drawn back to the way they saw you recruit them (over the Net) and want to do that and nothing else. So, you better be clear up front what you expect and what they should expect.

THE GREAT EQUALIZER

This is a biggie! The Internet is the great training equalizer. Instead of having some seventh-generation photocopy used as training material, consider a team-training site where everything is provided to build a business—everything you know, your upline knows, and their upline knows. This way, everyone has access to the same information no matter if you sponsored them or their next-door neighbor sponsored them.

Here is the scenario I have used to develop my training site. When I feel this requirement is met, I will feel my training site is complete:

A lady is really motivated and determined to make her brand-new Internet business work for her. Just two days ago, her brother signed her up, and she is fired up and ready to get going. She goes back and meets with her brother, and he barely knows how to order products, let alone build a business. His upline is nearly as uninformed. All of a sudden her big dreams seem almost impossible because she doesn't have a clue what to do. The next day a letter arrives in the mail from someone in her upline she has never heard of before. It tells her to log onto the Internet and check out their team's training site on how to build a business. She goes to the site and voila!"

Please realize I provided you with only the five-minute overview of this concept. However, it should give you an idea of the importance of a training system.

SOME OTHER THOUGHTS . . .

Use your site to generate local prospects. If you generate prospects all over the country (even the world), you will have a more difficult time trying to sponsor, train, manage, support, and motivate your team. You may even find that having far-away prospects prevents you from developing some basic business skills, such as how to give a presentation.

The Good and the Bad

Although it might appear that I have a bias against the Internet, I believe it offers enormous potential if used properly. However, many people are currently using and teaching about the Internet completely backwards. It is being used (and taught) as a complete business-building approach. The very essence of our business, the concept of simply recommending and promoting products and services through your network of acquaintances and relationships, is being removed from the process.

I feel that the people who can develop a system that incorporates the Internet into their current business-building system will reap huge rewards. There should be a system where the Internet enhances rather than replaces a distributor's ability to build a network and communicate information to their prospects and downline.

I also believe that over the next few years the Internet will have a large impact on training. In the near future, through the use of Real Audio, Real Video, and training Web sites, people will have access to vital, important information in real time. The ability to pass information down to many levels will become as simple as posting it on a Web site and sending out an e-mail to your downline distribution list. New IBOs will be able to log on to their computers, download a weekly training video, and then go out and apply the information they gained.

Most important, you will be able to go to your team's training site and look up exactly what you need help on—be it prospecting tips, presentation advice, personal development book recommendations, or whatever you need help with. It will be as if your upline leaders are personally working with you, sharing everything they have learned to reach the top.

These are exciting times as this new Information Age takes shape. For those out there who dream of being a pioneer, this is the time to seize the day.

Getting People Started—a 12-Month Plan

How do you keep your people motivated?

That's kind of a good news, bad news joke: The bad news is that you don't, and you can't. If people are relying on you for their motivation, then you have to continually pump them up, and who's going to pump them when you're not around?

On the other hand, the good news is that it isn't your responsibility to keep people motivated in the first place. It's better to be a leader and keep people in action, moving toward a goal and a reward they're committed to. This is the philosophy behind the 12-month plan.

The first step in creating an effective 12-month plan with your new IBO is to ask him or her, "Why are you doing this business? What purpose is it serving?" Have him really think about those questions, and be specific with his answers.

I know that he or she wants to make money. That's great, but why exactly? Is it because her job's a dead-end? Is it because she wants a choice with her career?

I believe that's what it's really about for people—being able to choose what we want to do. That's how I understand the term "financial freedom." This business can buy people a choice.

If you're helping someone in your group devise a 12-month plan, you want to find out where they're committed to going—and why. What they're committed to having—and why.

HOW TO SET GOALS

In the last year or so, I've come to the conclusion that people don't really work for goals. Instead, I believe that people work for the *rewards* that goals represent, and that's an important distinction in creating goals that will actually motivate people.

For example, Olympic athletes don't work for the gold medal. They're driven to get what it represents. It represents being the best, the winner, maybe even the Olympic and/or World Record Holder. In some countries, a gold medal represents a house, a better way of living, and more income. In the United States, it represents endorsements, the possibilities of getting into pro sports, and perhaps even movie and television opportunities. The value is not in the little piece of metal; it's in the honor, the glory, the recognition, the endorsements, and the money that the gold medal represents.

In Quixtar, we often make the mistake of working for a goal rather than a reward. People can't work for goals. I mean, $10,000 a month may be a goal, but so what? So you've got $10,000 a month. What's the $10,000 a month for? Does it represent being able to afford a better house? Does it mean that now you can leave the $60,000 a year job that you don't like? Does it represent a better education for your children?

People need to think about what rewards their goals represent. Then, you can set two kinds of rewards with them: a long-term reward, something they will enjoy long past attaining the goal, and a reward they give themselves as soon as they reach the goal.

Have you ever noticed how hard people work for prizes? Even if the prize is nothing more than recognition. The intention here is to have every step, every income goal, in the entire 12-month project be directly linked to a prize.

STRUCTURING THE PLAN

Because income is the most tangible measure of progress, I always set income goals first. In any compensation plan, you can figure that X amount of volume at Y percentage equals Z amount of income. So, income goals provide the backbone of your distributor's plan.

Another benefit of creating income goals is that it clarifies people's expectations. Many people come into this business with visions of sugar plum dollars dancing in their heads. They rarely have matching visions about what work they'll need to do to get those plums. Vague but shiny expectations set people up for disappointment.

So, you begin by doing the math, starting with the 12-month mark. Decide how much income your distributor is going for and associate that number with the amount of volume needed to create it.

Next, divide that figure by a number of key leaders. Let's say we plan for five key leaders, since that number works well in almost any plan.

Let's assume that $200,000 of volume per month, divided by five key leaders, equals $40,000 per leader per month in volume. That $200,000 of volume at, say, four percent pays $8,000 a month.

Once you calculate 12 months of income in terms of volume and leaders, then you go all the way back to the beginning, to the first 30 days.

SETTING THE 30-DAY GOAL

I believe there are seven components to a 30-day goal: Intended Result, Reward, Conditions of Satisfaction, Milestones, Single Daily Action, Hot Team, and What's Next. You'll notice that some of these components are ways to break the journey into smaller and smaller steps. I call it eating the elephant one bite at a time. An important component to success is to review and report with your upline leader at the end of every 30 days. This will keep you on track.

Intended result

Look at the year's goal and ask, "What are you going to put in place this month that's going to advance you toward that goal?"

Note that the first couple of months are predominately structural, they're not really for earning income. Your IBOs are laying the foundation for what they're going to be building over the course of the next year. A good example of an intended result for the first 30-day goal would be to have two of your IBOs' five key leaders in the business.

Each 30-day goal needs to put them one step closer to the 12-month goal. Each month builds on the one before. A person's intended result must be specific and measurable, so he'll know exactly what to build upon in the next 30 days.

Reward

She's set her goal, so what's the reward? Every 30 days, you have a reward attached to a goal. The reward doesn't need to be extravagant, but it needs to be significant to your IBO, and she needs to be as committed to the reward as she is to the goal—maybe even more so.

Set a reward so that she has this little prize at the end: an outfit she picked out because it looked fun to wear, a romantic dinner with her spouse, 24 hours of guilt-free loafing, a marathon manicure. Just make sure it's something that really is a treat, something that she's going to look forward to that's worth the commitment.

Conditions of satisfaction

The next component: if the goal is to find two key leaders in the business by the end of the month, then you have to determine the conditions of satisfaction. What are the criteria for a key leader? What does a key leader look like? Does your new IBO meet the criteria? Do you?

I have people articulate their conditions for someone to be considered a key leader. You might define it by whether or not the key leader purchases a certain amount of product when she starts the business, or maybe she already has an idea of where she wants to go. Is her attitude right? Is she committed? Does the key leader know people, and has she made a list of contacts and prospects? Is she following the system training?

If your IBO is clear on his conditions of satisfaction, then when he's going through the sorting process, he can make decisions based on each prospect's characteristics and how she fits his strategy for success. The purpose is not to put anyone down, but to make it easier for your people to determine when they actually have the kind of leader they're looking for.

When I put people in the business, the first thing we do after they've done their paperwork is set up what I call "orientation." Orientation is where I coach them though this entire system in a one-hour meeting or phone call. During the orientation, I tell them that most of this system has come from the success training of my own upline. Often people don't have much structure to what they are building, and they don't know why they're building it. I think that's why people get caught up in the get-rich-quick or lottery mentality.

I teach them to see this as methodology that requires work and discipline. I tell people up front that if you want productivity and you want income in this business, I haven't found a way in 20 years to do it without hard work. One of my conditions of satisfaction for someone in my organization is that the person must be willing to work. I also look for commitment. If someone lacks those two qualities, then he or she will probably make a better friend than a business partner.

Milestones

Milestones are "by whens." Using the same example, if my IBO is going to get two key leaders in the business in the first 30 days, by when will she have her list of candidates? By when will she have talked to at least 10 people on the list? By when will she have selected the best five? By when will she have put two of the five in the business?

You see, this way, in a four-week structure, your distributor can have her prospect list and make contacts, knowing which milestone she'll need to reach each week—"This is what I'm going to do this week. This is what I'm going to do next week."—and so on. It's a natural progression toward the end.

Single daily action

The next piece is the single daily action, which, for these purposes, is defined as something you commit to do each and every day that is easy, fun, and contributes to the intended result of the month.

For instance, your IBO has a prospect list with 100 names on it. A good single daily action would be to speak directly to five people on the list. I don't care if it's the same people two days in a row. Just speak to someone on that prospect list about the business every day, five days a week. You know he may have to make more than one call to reach someone directly, but have him keep calling until he does, because answering machines don't count as conversations.

If you find that your distributor's single daily action is something he dreads doing, or an action that doesn't move him toward his goal, then change it. A single daily action is a tool, not a punishment or chore.

Dream team

The "dream team" concept is something that I think is badly needed in this business, because most people have only their sponsor for support, and 95 percent of the time they don't get what they need. I request that everyone develop a dream team—a four- or five-person structure for support. Team members can be upline and downline, it doesn't matter.

Now, these are five people whom your distributor enrolls in what she's doing and who agree to be available to her when she needs support. She also has to make being on her dream team a request that people can decline without offending her. You can't force people to support you—it won't work. Once people agree to be on your distributor's dream team, their responsibility is to be there for her and not to criticize. Their job is to be a cheerleader, to be supportive, and to listen.

A dream team gives people a place to go for support when their sponsor is unavailable for whatever reason. However, you may want to be on your IBO's dream team, and that's fine too.

What's next?

The last component is "What's next?"

For a long time, I've believed that goals need to lived as inevitabilities, that the more inevitable they are, the more surely they will happen. I feel that defining "What's next?" after the goal is achieved is a great way to reinforce that idea: "I'm committed to reaching this goal in this time-frame; therefore, what's the next step after I've accomplished that?"

When people are setting their first 30-day goal, I ask them to also be thinking about what the 60-day goal is, but only as a sketch. When this is complete, what will the next step be? That way, when they get close to the end of the first month, they're already clear about what they're going to be doing next, and it makes it easier for them to set up the next 30-day goal.

SIX-MONTH CHECK POINT

After six months, we do a comprehensive evaluation. "What do you think about your 12-month goal now that you're at the halfway point?"

To prepare, have your IBO note, in the very beginning, where he needs to be in six months to be on track. It's his six-month checkpoint. You can tell very quickly whether a person's ahead or behind the pace for reaching their goal.

If I'm putting my own team in place, my second month's goal is to get the next two key leaders in the business, plus help the first two get their first key leaders. Then I know what I have to do to ensure that I'm on track when my six-month check point comes around.

If your distributor's goal is to make $10,000 a month at the end of a year, what does his level of income need to be at the end of six months?

For that goal, most people need an income somewhere between $3,000 and $5,000. If it's a little lower, it's probably still okay because of how effort duplicates—for example, if you have five people earning $2,000 a month and it takes you six months to earn $2,000 a month, you could spend the next six months getting there, and that's going to cinch $10,000 for you.

THE RESULTS

To me, the most exciting part of this 12-month plan is the way it makes lights go on all over the place for people. For once they can actually see how their success is going to happen.

Usually in this business, too much is left to the imagination, too few steps are mapped out between the starting line and the goal. Most people get into business to make more money, no matter how enthusiastic they are about a product. But when you get right down to it, most people never stop and think about what "more money" really looks like, or what they're willing to do on a daily basis to make "more money" happen.

I've noticed that there are tons of people in our business that spend a lot of money and work very hard on their businesses without getting anywhere. I think that's because, when people don't have a structure for what they're building, they don't know what they're committed to accomplishing or how to do it—and neither do the people they're putting in the business! Everybody's excited, but the steps to reaching their goals are vague at best. When they write out a monthly course of action toward a specific result, and the tasks along the way are rewarded, they win every month! They're never disappointed by an $800.00 check, because that's an expected milestone in the plan.

Once people feel like they are on track to attain the rewards represented by their goals, they stay in the business.

Communication, support, and follow-up are the keys to making the 12-month plan really work.

There are many ways to skin the Internet business cat and make money, and this isn't the only way. But it is a way I've found that works 100 percent of the time if it's done consistently. There's almost no way to do it wrong either—except not to do it.

I've learned that people have a very deep need to contribute, and this is a way for them to not only succeed themselves but also to effectively teach and coach others to be productive. That's a wonderful gift to be able to give. It's part of what makes this system so powerful and effective.

When you give people something that holds them accountable, they start to hold themselves accountable and discover their own strengths and abilities. You reach something deep in people by looking for all that they can be and giving them the gift of themselves. People have a need to give and contribute and to be loved as a result, and this 12-month plan is a simple, proven system for achieving that.

ACTION SUMMARY

Now, let's review:

1. Articulate exactly why you're in business. Where are you committed to going, what are you committed to having, and *why*?
2. Set your 12-month goals. How much do you plan to earn by the 12th month, and what rewards does that figure represent?
3. Structure your 12-month plan. Start with month 12 and determine, according to our compensation plan, how much volume between how many leaders you will need to produce to hit your goal. Do the math all the way back to the first month.
4. Set your 30-day goal. You want to determine the result you hope to achieve for that 30 days and the actions needed to attain that result. Plan a reward for yourself if your goal is achieved. The conditions of satisfaction, in other words the criteria for leaders to have in order to expedite the sorting process, should be set forth in advance. In addition, set milestones, or "by whens," within the month so you know exactly what you need to do every day. Select a dream team, a four- or five-person support structure for your business efforts. Know "What's next?"—the next step you'll need to take after you reach your goal so that you're clear and "ready to rock" when the time comes.
5. Establish a six-month checkpoint. In the beginning, note where you need to be at six months to reach the 12-month goal. After six months, do a comprehensive evaluation. If you need to, adjust the action plan. If you're on track, keep going and you'll reach the finish line!

Five Top Tips for Telephone Invitations

Using these will increase your effectiveness tremendously. They are:

1. "Is this a good time?"
2. Transfer enthusiasm.
3. Compliment your prospect.
4. Offer a disclaimer.
5. Close your objective.

There are also some common issues that arise when inviting people over the phone:

1. "I'm busy."
2. "I'm not interested."
3. Keeping in touch.
4. Another approach—ask for advice.

Keeping these issues in mind will ultimately enable you to:

5. Learn to love your telephone.

Let's talk about each one of them:

"IS THIS A GOOD TIME?"

Have you ever had someone call you when you didn't want to talk? What kind of reception did you give them? How well did you listen and how open were you to what they were saying? We've all had it happen. So, point one, find out if this is a good time to talk. It's an appreciated courtesy, and what's more, it makes sure you get the listening you deserve.

TRANSFER ENTHUSIASM

Most people think that communication is a transfer of information from one person to the next. And for limited purposes, it is. But truly effective communication requires transferring enthusiasm not just information. What you say is certainly important. But I believe that how you feel about what you say is the most important thing of all.

You don't have to become an expert about all the facts and features of your product, your company, or your marketing plan to be a powerful communicator. In fact, being that kind of expert may actually block real and effective communication.

Please remember that this is the duplication business. It's far easier to learn to share enthusiasm than to attempt to transfer years of acquired knowledge. The more excited and enthusiastic you are, the more likely and quickly you'll be successful. Again, the key to the word *enthusiasm* is the last four letters: I-A-S-M—"I am sold myself." You have to be your own best customer! If you find more and more people aren't interested in your product or opportunity, look first to your own enthusiasm. I'll bet it's begun to wane.

You know, there's an old sales adage that says that when you first start out, you're 90 percent enthusiasm and 10 percent knowledge. After a while it changes to 90 percent knowledge and 10 percent enthusiasm. Just before that time, either you do something to increase that enthusiasm percentage, or you should start looking for another product or service to work with.

COMPLIMENT YOUR PROSPECTS

The reason it is important to compliment your prospects is that when you do so over the phone, you accomplish two things. First, you have now set clearly in their minds why it was so important for you to contact them. And second, you really have their attention! Do you listen any differently to someone who calls you and starts talking about what they want to say versus someone who calls you and says he or she really values your opinion because you're such a professional, or because you have such a great sense of quality or good taste? It works.

OFFER A DISCLAIMER

How many times have people tried to sell you something by selling you, selling you, selling you, selling you! The more pushy they are, the more you shut down. It's natural. We all do it for protection, if nothing else. Allow your prospects to feel there is no obligation in meeting with you. Give your prospect the space to let his or her natural curiosity come to the fore. And let them know this isn't for everybody. That'll get their interest up.

CLOSE YOUR OBJECTIVE

The last point is to get what you want from the call. If your objective is to set an appointment, offer your prospect a choice of times and days you know would be good for him to meet with you. Don't ask him, "When can we get together?" If your objective is to send him a promo package or a sample, then assume that's what he wants. Tell him what you're going to do and ask him where he wants you to send it. Always come from the assumption that your prospects want what you have to offer. When you do that, more often than not they will.

Now, let's give an example of how these five ingredients all blend together.

"Hi, Betty, this is Cynthia Copier. Is this a convenient time for us to talk for a couple of minutes? It is? Great!

"Betty, the reason I'm calling is that I'm so excited about something I just got involved with. I thought of you because of the way people feel about you and respect you. I know you can do extremely well with this.

"Now I can't make any guarantees, Betty. I'm not completely sure this is something that's right for you. What I would like to do is just sit down together for a few minutes and share some ideas. I think you'll see a fantastic opportunity here. I believe you'll see ways we can have a lot of fun with this and how we can make a lot of money together.

"So, I'm buying lunch this week, Betty. Which day is best for you, Tuesday or Thursday?"

Now, that has all of the five ingredients you want in a call.

I recommend that you prepare a script for the calls you're going to make—not to sound like a computer but rather to write down an outline of those key points: why you're calling her (why Betty is important to you), why it may not be right for her, what you want to do, and finally, give her a choice of when to get together.

With a simple outline of a script in front of you, you don't have to exert effort to remember what you're going to say. You can focus on transferring your enthusiasm.

Common Objections and How to Handle Them

Now, you're frequently going to be asked some questions. If someone asks you, "What is it?" my strong recommendation is to tell them. Don't try to avoid that question!

Tell the prospect the name of the company, the name of the product, and be prepared to give a one- or two-sentence description of what the company does or what the product is, and then go right back into closing your objective. Don't rush this either. Avoiding the answer or sounding like you wish they'd never asked isn't a good message to communicate.

If you're genuinely enthusiastic, you'll gladly answer and move along to what you really want to talk about. If you're not, your prospect will pick it up for sure. People have a built-in insincerity alarm. It goes off loud and clear when it hears avoidance.

The most valuable quality you have in this industry is your integrity and your word. So when you're asked a question, answer it straight, short, and true—and then move forward once again to your objective.

"I'M BUSY."

You might get a response such as, "Well, I don't know, Cynthia, I'm very busy . . . I don't think I'd be interested in this." Then you can say: "Betty, I can definitely appreciate that. I know you're busy. That's one reason why I called you. You're the kind of woman who gets things done. Look, Betty, if you don't see within a matter of 20 or 25 minutes something that really excites you, I promise I won't bring it up to you again. So I'm still buying lunch. Which day is best for you, Tuesday or Thursday?"

And if she doesn't see any value after your presentation, don't pressure her.

Keep your word with people.

"I'M NOT INTERESTED."

Okay, here's what you do with this one. Find out, specifically, what it is that doesn't interest them. Ask a question like: "Betty, I can appreciate that. Just for my benefit, would you tell me what part of this it is that you're not interested in? Is it the product and the benefits it offers? Is it the business opportunity?"

Now, if they, your prospects, say it's the business opportunity, you can tell them you understand and encourage them to give the product a try, based on the benefits you're excited about along with your money-back guarantee.

However, sometimes a statement like this is a smoke screen for something else. Maybe it's a difficult time for them in their lives. Perhaps they are one of the people who's had a problem with a "bad" or inappropriate opportunity in our industry. Whatever it is, do your best to pin down what they're not interested in and why.

If they are flat out not interested at all, that's fine. Give them room to be that way. Do not pressure them! And always leave an opening to get back in touch.

KEEPING IN TOUCH

"Well, Betty, I understand that you're not interested now. But I really value your opinion, so I'd like to keep in touch with you. Would you be open to me calling you again and letting you know how I'm doing maybe a month or so down the road?" Get a commitment from this person that they would have no objection with your keeping in touch. Most of the time, a "not interested" response simply means that the timing is not right for the person. Nothing convinces someone like success does—as you become more successful, they may become more open. The time may be right for the prospect sooner than either of you imagined.

And remember, we're in the sorting business. So, the rule of thumb is: some will, some won't, so what—NEXT!

Keeping in communication with people is a real key to your success. Many times a distributor has approached me when the timing just wasn't right for me. But he or she kept in touch. And often, after a couple months, I was more open to what he or she had to offer.

And it's true: people love to share each other's success. Just hearing about somebody who's doing really well picks me up and makes me smile. Make sure to keep the lines of communication open and share your success with people. It's powerful!

Some experts say that people don't respond until the fourth or fifth contact. I don't know if that's completely accurate, but I do know that persistence and what I call "relentless patience" pays off again and again. This is a classic case of "Just Do It."

Also, always, no matter what the outcome of the call, thank your prospect. Thank her for her opinion, thank her for her support, and thank her for her valuable time. Pay her a compliment if you can. This is a sure-fire way to have her be happy to hear from you the next time you try to call.

ANOTHER APPROACH—ASK FOR ADVICE

A very successful way to introduce someone to an opportunity, and one that beautifully combines all of the key ingredients, is to ask for the person's advice. This works particularly well with family members, friends, and even acquaintances whose background or experience make their opinions valuable. Simply tell the person that you're considering starting or have just started your own business, and you want to show him or her your product or opportunity to get an opinion. People love to give advice, especially if you elevate them to the position of being an expert on the subject. Chances are, they'll see the value you see in your product and/or opportunity. Now your "expert" just became your customer or distributor!

I recommend that you prepare one basic phone script for family and close friends, and another for acquaintances and people you don't know that well. You just choose different words for the different categories of prospects.

LEARN TO LOVE YOUR TELEPHONE

A wise person once said, "The speed by which we manifest the things we want in life is directly proportionate to the speed with which we become comfortable with those things." The sooner you make a friend of that "user-friendly" phone of yours, the sooner you'll be able to use its awesome power to build your business with the greatest success. Make a commitment to call a specific number of prospects per day, per week, per month—and do it! You'll be amazed how light that phone becomes in just a couple of days or weeks. One thing I strongly suggest is to get a phone you really like and enjoy using. There are all kinds of terrific new phones available now.

Beyond the Chicken and the Egg

I learned this from the late John Kalench, a motivational speaker and author. He talks about which comes first—the chicken or the egg? You know the dilemma: When you want to invite someone to take a look at your network marketing business, what do you show them first, your product or your opportunity? People teach all different kinds of answers to that question. My answer is: Don't show them the chicken *or* the egg. First, tell them about farming itself. And, of course, "farming" is network marketing.

Let me explain.

It's important to focus your marketing efforts on the needs of the marketplace out there—not on what *you* think that's of value, but on what people are truly looking for.

In today's economic climate, what do people need most? In their eyes, people don't need nutritional products, weight-loss products, skin care products, or water-treatment products. The truth is, no matter what a fantastic egg you have, or, for that matter, how great a chicken, neither one is really what people are looking for. Today, more than at any other time in our history, what people need are financial alternatives. They need an opportunity to make money in a way that they have control of their financial future. No matter how good your product or how terrific your particular company, what people need most from you is to hear about the opportunity offered by network marketing itself.

BEYOND THE "JOB"

Faced with today's uncertain economics, most people still think in terms of looking for a "job." The first thing you need to do is to make a dent in that habitual way of thinking by showing them that "the job" is not the answer, that their ongoing success depends on them, because "job security" is going the way of the dinosaurs. Open their minds to the possibility of taking control of their own financial future without depending on "a job." Introduce them to the concept of taking control of their lives through this marvelous industry called Network Marketing.

The crucial element of this context is that you're not attempting to "sell" anything here: You're out to offer information, knowledge, and an education.

"I'm looking for a handful of people who are fed up—who have gotten to the point where they want to take control of their own futures, who are no longer simply in the market for a job, but are looking for a way to determine what happens to them, personally and professionally. There's an industry out there that allows you to do that. Here's what, in essence, you should tell your prospects:

"I've got some incredible information that explains exactly what this industry is and what it can do for you. I'm not here to sell you anything; I'm here to inform you about a financial alternative. I'd like to share this information with you for a short period of time. I can give it to you for only about 48 hours, because I have so many other people who want to look over this information.

"At the end of those 48 hours, if you see a value in this and want to look further at specific possibilities, then I'd love to sit down with you and share some details about the particular products and company that I'm involved with right now. But first, I want to share with you this generic information about the fantastic alternative that this industry offers."

WHY IS THIS THE BEST APPROACH?

For three reasons: First, because of today's economic climate, it hits us squarely between the eyes. We absolutely must be aware of what people are going through out there.

Second, because people are tired of being sold. They're being sold all the time, constantly—on the TV, in the papers, on their phone at dinnertime, on billboards on the way to work . . . sold, sold, sold. Give them a break! Approach them differently. Don't try to sell them anything, and let them know that right up front, that there are no strings attached to your offer to educate them.

The third and strongest reason is that by approaching new people this way, you connect them to the big picture first. Rather than showing them the specifics of your product and your company, you're connecting them to the process itself.

Then, when you sit down to "sell" them on the specifics of your products and company, they're already "sold"! When they are already aware of the process, then they'll have a sense (subconsciously, if nothing else) that they will want your products and your specific opportunity to work for them. They will truly sell themselves.

ARE YOU CREATING A POSITIVE "BELIEF SYSTEM"?

Yes—and no. In a sense, you're helping create a positive belief with people who *want* to have that belief. But you're not really creating it. If anything, you're unleashing a positive belief system that was waiting to be born, so to speak. You're tapping into people's desire for an alternative and showing them a solution. You're giving them hope and finding out which people are ready to make a change, and which people are not.

Remember—and this is important—you're not trying to convince people of the value of network marketing! You're aware of the economic climate, and you know they are too. You're coming from a place of pure contribution—not "pretending" to do so, but really doing so. That's all you need to do! You're letting this information get into their hands, and then letting them make a choice as to whether or not they want to look into it further.

If they're not open to the financial alternative of network marketing, nothing prevents you from still sharing your product with them—you've lost nothing. And if they are open, by connecting them to the process first, you've increased your chances of sponsoring a real business builder and not simply a wholesale product user.

WHAT KIND OF TOOLS?

Using "generic" tools—information that educates and inspires people about network marketing, but which does not come from your particular company, is central to this type of selling approach.

Today, there are a good number of generic tools available. Some people use books, others use audiotapes, others like to rely on videos. What's the most effective approach? What you really need are two tools—because there are two different tasks you want to fulfill: to inspire and to inform.

Inspire—then inform.

It's been proven over and over that the written word is the most powerful way to give people facts, to inform people.

When people see something in print, they believe more strongly that it's true. So you'll want to use a book about network marketing to convey solid, professional information about this industry that people will believe.

But no matter how good or how interesting the book, the fact is that most people will not invest the hour or two to sit down and read a book unless their interest is already piqued. So the other needed step is to give them a tool that will compel them to read the book—and the medium of videotape is perfectly suited for that purpose.

A video is a powerful way to reach people's emotions—not their logic, but their emotions, which in turn can influence them to take action. Now, to some extent, an audiotape can do that as well. An audio does not convey images as powerfully as a good video; on the other hand, it can be listened to in the car and doesn't require that the person set aside the short time it takes to sit down in their living room and view it. Both video and audio have their strong points. In the balance, I favor video because of its more compelling, powerful impact.

Sometimes people try to use a video to fully educate people about our industry, but the fact is you really can't answer the major questions people have about network marketing effectively with videotape. Explaining key concepts, such as the duplication principle or the idea of geometric growth, is far easier to do on paper than on a video.

By combining these two media, video and book, you can have the greatest impact and make the most difference, giving you the greatest chance to get into that person's mind so they think, "This is really a viable thing, I should really give this a serious look."

At Millionaires in Motion, for example, we've created a set of generic tools—a short book on network marketing and a 23-minute video filled with powerful testimonials from people in all walks of life—that are designed specifically to complement each other in this way. We call it "The Prospector's Kit."

The two items work together to stimulate, inspire, and educate. People watch the video first, and then, if that involves them emotionally and piques their interest in the possibilities, they become motivated enough to sit down and read through the book, which gives them enough facts and information to justify their excitement.

THE PROCESS *IS* THE PRODUCT

Successful people in this industry are those who love the industry itself as much as, or even more than, their own products and particular company. They love the process. They push through any failure, any disappointment or discouragement they encounter, and they keep pushing until they find the right vehicle for them. And that's because they're connected to the process itself, more than to a particular product. They are the ones who find the company of their dreams and then make it big in this industry.

Since that's true, what better way to introduce a new person than to sit down with them—before you show them the chicken or the egg—and connect them with the process itself!

The Wizard of Oz

Most of you know how powerful belief is. Attempting to change those old patterns or beliefs is not a one-time effort. One attempt doesn't make a belief—ask any smoker who is trying to quit. It takes repetition. It is the reiteration of the visualization that changes the neurons of your brain.

Too many of you keep waiting for permission to unleash the potential inside of you. Too many of you wait for someone else to affirm you, to give you the right to do something. By changing your belief, what you really know to be true about yourself, you will change your performance. You and your performance match your image of reality.

Beliefs are powerful, as shown by the fact that a placebo, a sugar pill, can cure an ailment. You believe the doctor, the chemist, or the surgeon. They give you the medication, and your body heals, often times because of your belief. Well, if you can get well on a positive placebo, could you get sick on a negative placebo? Who are you listening to? Who are your children listening to? Who are your people in your company listening to? Who is telling them "the truth?" You must be careful who and what you listen to.

Nearly every one of you has seen the movie *The Wizard of Oz*. When I was a little girl, growing up in Texas, I was mesmerized by this show. I dreamt of being swept away and of making my dreams come true. Anyone else felt the same way? Dorothy and Toto get whisked out of Kansas inside a tornado, and must find the Wizard of Oz in order to get home. Along the way, they meet the Scarecrow, the Tin Man, and the Cowardly Lion. (Perhaps like some people you know! The one without brains . . . the one without a heart . . . the one with no courage.)

All of them set off to find the Wizard, the all-powerful, along the yellow brick road. Each of them needed something from the Wizard: The Scarecrow wanted a brain, the Tin Man a heart, and the Cowardly Lion wanted courage. And Dorothy, she just wanted to go home. Through the apple-throwing trees and flying monkeys, the Wicked Witch of the West, all the trials and challenges of getting to the Wizard, Dorothy's companions proved that they already had what they thought they needed. They just didn't believe it!

It took the Wizard, one of the biggest fakes of all time, to affirm what each already had. He bestowed a diploma on the Scarecrow, who, all of a sudden, had brains; a clock on the Tin Man, so he could hear the heart he already had; and a medal on the Cowardly Lion, to represent the courage he had already shown. Dorothy discovered that she possessed the ability to get home all along. She was actually wearing this ability, in the form of the ruby slippers on her feet.

Dorothy and the others always had what they thought they needed. Somebody else had to affirm them. Luckily, Dorothy and the others met a positive wizard. However, you may have run into too many negative wizards who tried to take your heart, your brains, or your hope. They may have been teachers, coaches, drama teachers, grandparents, or spouses. For some, this is even directed toward their entire culture or race.

What happens if you gave sanction to what they said? You need to release yourself from those old beliefs. Look now at your own future and don't talk yourself out of it! You are ready to take on the responsibility. It is all right to start your own business, to take on more and grow. It is all right to be successful. It is all right to be free, happy, and healthy. Free yourselves, and those of you who have children, teach your children, too. Watch out for the negative wizards. Don't buy into it. Beware of those who need to tell you "the truth."

One more thing: Remember the song in the Wizard of Oz? "I'm off to see the Wizard, the wonderful Wizard of Oz." Instead of saying, "I'm off to see the Wizard," from now forward say, "I'm off to *be* the Wizard, the wonderful Wizard of Oz." You know why? "I'm off to be the Wizard, because of the wonderful things *I* 'does'!"

Now go, do, and be—all the things you *used* to think were impossible!

I believe in you!

Cynthia Stewart-Copier
www.DaretoDreamBig.com

APPENDIX C

Conversations with Dexter Yager

Dexter Yager is arguably one of the most powerful distributors in the history of network marketing. He built his organization on the simple concept that people need an ongoing stream of inspiration, motivation, instruction, encouragement, and information on personal growth each and every month to instill belief in themselves, their profession, and their company (and its products). This belief translates into commitment, loyalty, persistency, and a personal version of success. Dexter transmuted this approach into an organization the size of a small country, complete with the accompanying wealth. Join me, Cynthia Stewart-Copier (CSC), as I interview him—to get an inside look at the man, his success, his vision, and his mission.

CSC: *"Dexter, you are an icon in this industry, a legend. Tell me, who is Dexter Yager?"*

DY: I am just an ordinary guy, with extraordinary dreams. Birdie and I came from a small mill town. Birdie was the youngest of 14 children. Most of the people we knew were broke, living paycheck to paycheck, working at a local mill or at a state institution. We didn't know anyone who had big dreams, or especially talked about them. There didn't seem to be a single big thinker among our friends. I was ridiculed for the dreams and goals I had. "What makes you think you'll ever amount to anything Dexter?" they'd say. "You don't have an education and you don't know anything about business. You're never going to make it."

It was hard to hear those put-downs, especially from everyone you were closest to. It stops most people from succeeding. Their concerns with what their friends and families think are greater than their concerns about their family's future. I wasn't going to let my neighbors or coworkers take away my dreams or the possibilities for my family's future. A true friend is an encourager. A discourager is your enemy. They will kill you, or at least a part of you, if you let them kill your dreams. Friends find things that are right about you, about your hopes or goals, and even if they don't join in your dreams, they encourage them, they encourage you.

CSC: *"Dexter, you have accomplished an enormous success in network marketing. Tell me how you got started and why you stuck with it through the past 35 years."*

DY: I got in my own business as an Amway distributor over 35 years ago. In the beginning, my biggest dream was to make an extra $1,000 a month. That money would allow me to quit my job and work my own business full time. It was as far as I could see in the early days. As I reached each goal, I set another one, a bigger one. That way I was always reaching, always looking forward. If you aren't moving forward, you are going backwards. I learned that lesson early on. That is why I am always talking to my leaders about getting a big dream and keeping it out in front of you everyday.

I stuck with it because it made sense. There is simply nothing else out there that comes close to the advantages we have with

Quixtar or with Amway. We have the history and the numbers to prove it.

I could have made hundreds of millions of dollars by starting my own company years ago—but I didn't! People have enough confusion to handle. I didn't want to create more. I wanted my people to know they could trust me—and they do! People need to be able to trust others; their upline, product lines, and company.

My expertise is loving the people and caring about them. I teach people to take responsibility for themselves and empower them to stretch and reach beyond where they thought they could.

It is the books and tapes that teach people how to empower themselves and to achieve success in both their business and their personal lives. This system of books and tapes allows others to help their people, giving them the same opportunities to achieve success. We have the greatest personal development program that teaches people to realize their potential and empowers them to achieve success. We call it *the system.*

CSC: "*Tell me more about this system of personal development.*"

DY: I realized that if I love my wife and kids, and I want to give them total freedom, I have to give others the opportunity to have theirs.

The system is really teaching people to be their own leader. It is teaching people to realize the potential within them and gives them the information to act and develop financially strong businesses. The system allows people to be independent. My leaders only counsel with me when they have questions or they want to report and review their progress. But they think for themselves. They choose to take the suggestions or not. They are the ones that create successful businesses.

When I work with someone, I am constantly investing in his or her future, both financially and with my time, which is worth a lot! I drive my own car to help them, pay my own expenses, use my own training materials, etc. If they quit, I am the one that loses. I am the one who has made the investment.

I want to empower others to build their own big businesses. When I do they win big! If you understand our compensation plan, when I help someone else reach Platinum, they are earning 25 percent. My compensation for helping them is 4 percent, and it is not even paid by them, the company pays it.

CSC: *"Dexter, in your opinion, what is the reason many people fail?"*

DY: The challenge with most people is that they have poor self-esteem. Their self-image is low and it is easy for them to get comfortable in a lifestyle that is far below their capabilities. It is also easy for them to stay there because so many of the people around them are in the same boat and they are all constantly affirming their limitations.

But leaders create their own reality. Leaders change the way they think about themselves and others. They don't accept mediocrity. They have big dreams and the courage to work to make those dreams a reality.

The path to success is having a solid foundation to run on. People fail because of lack of knowledge. We have never had a failure in Amway. We just had people that quit! How could they have failed? They quit! They never even found out if they would have made it or not.

Success is a struggle. Every prophet in the Bible struggled; had trials and tribulations. I hear some people say, "This can't be of God. God would have made it easier!"

God wants to develop you into a leader. Leaders don't come from the welfare system—a free ride. Just look at Moses, Job, Joseph, or Jesus. Each dealt with more struggles or challenges than anyone of us ever has. All of God's top men and women had incredible obstacles to hurdle, why would we expect less of ourselves? I believe that it is in the struggle that we become strong.

When I was a boy, I grew up in a mill town. The majority of the town was blue collar and most of them worked at the mill, or a related industry. Now, I don't think there is anything wrong with that, but I wanted something different. I took a lot of criticism from my friends. "What makes you think you can make it in business? You don't have an education. You don't have any money. And you stutter! Who do you think you are anyway?" I heard again and again. I could have let that stop me. Many people do let the criticism and ridicule of their friends or coworkers stop them from believing in their dreams. I didn't.

CSC: *"Dexter, what gave you the incentive to develop this successful program you call 'The System?'"*

DY: Thirty-five years ago I signed up in Amway. I worked really hard and reached the level of direct, now referred to as Platinum, in that first year. I was able to quit my job and continue to build my business full time. However, in the following three years, my business leveled off, and soon I realized that I was even going backwards. Something was terribly wrong! But what?

After evaluating my business and the turn it had taken, I realized where I had gone wrong. In the beginning, I stretched others, encouraging them, working with them, and promoting the business until I got my dream, which was to quit my job and devote myself full time to my own business. When I reached that goal, I settled in. I got too comfortable. My people had no one to follow, No one to hold the torch and lead the way.

I learned a valuable lesson through this setback—keep a big dream in front of you. I think we should all set long-term goals and short-term goals. But when you are about to hit that goal, make sure you have set another one out ahead. Always be looking forward.

Another thing I learned is that people need a way to duplicate themselves. I can't be with all of my leaders every single day, so I created a way that I could be there—training tapes. While I cannot physically train hundreds of people across the country in the same day, training tapes make that possible. For a nominal expense, anyone can have the training that I developed and practiced which made me successful. I expanded that idea into a tremendous training system that gives every person an equal opportunity to succeed by using the tips and advice from other extremely successful leaders in my business.

Some people that I sponsor are smarter than I am in their respective fields, but not in this business. They need to learn how to develop this kind of business. When I need information or help—let's say financial or health related—I seek experts to help me. I take their advice and utilize their expertise. A great example is my trainer at the gym. David is walking proof that he has the expertise I was looking for. He is a success in the fitness business. I am not. When I began my fitness program, I sought his advice. He taught me the things I needed to *know* and the things I needed to *do* to reach my personal health goals. Because I was willing to trust him and follow his advice, I am able to do things today I never imaged. In other words, I followed his system, and it worked!

CSC: "*Some people say that only the ones who get in business at the beginning make it big. Or they say that those who achieved success were lucky. How would you define success?*"

DY: Cynthia, success is not luck, nor is it a gift. I define success as work and failure. Birdie and I are the biggest failures in the business. We have failed more times than anyone else I know. People often ask me what the success ratio is in my business. I tell them the truth—it is 100 percent. One hundred percent of the people that are willing to keep working and keep failing make it!

The success ratio in our business is related to the number of people in one's organization. Birdie and I have lost more people than we have today, but each time we lost one, we learned to do things better. So, in the end, our losses were wins.

Take marriage for example. The longest running marriages are those that have had the most challenges. A newlywed couple couldn't comprehend the challenges they will face down the road. The longer they are married, the more they learn to respect the other person. If you show respect, you get respect. Take my kids as an example. I show my kids respect for the things they do right. I can't demand their respect, love, or recognition. I have to earn it. My children reciprocate what they see, what they have been taught.

Success is the same. However, even when you have earned the right to have respect, sometimes you still won't get it. Success is a terrible thing when it happens to the other guy. If your associates and family members chose to not get involved in your business and you make it big, they have to make up an excuse as to why they didn't do it—why they aren't successful. They have to justify their own failures.

So what is success? It is the golden touch—fail yourself to success! Work, fail, pull yourself up, work, fail, and do it all over again. If people would only look at their businesses like they look at their little kids. Remember when a toddler first starts to walk? They take those first wobbly steps and then, splat! They fall on their behinds. Do we run to those kids and say, "Okay honey, just stop trying to walk? It's too hard, too painful." No! We know they will eventually learn to do it right. It never occurs to us that they might not learn to walk. We expect they will, and they do. Now, as they are all grown up, do we remember those falls? No!

CSC: *"What do you feel are the steps to winning?"*

DY: In a race, the obvious winner should be the one with the longest legs. But most often the winner is the one who beats the odds! The facts don't count when a winner makes a decision. The past doesn't count. The odds don't count.

I think the first step to success is to change your thinking. Change it from failure mentality to a winning mentality. When you change your thinking, you change your life.

The next step is finding a mentor. Find a person who has achieved what you want to achieve, ask him for advice, and then *do* what he has told you. For example, when I go to the gym, I don't argue with my trainer. I do the exercises he gives me and eat the diet he suggests. I want a piece of what he has. I take his advice and trust him because I can see the results when I look at him.

So when you are looking for a mentor, look for the fruit on the tree. Does this person exemplify success or do they have the results you are looking for? In health and fitness, or in business, this recipe for success is the same. A person cannot teach what they don't *do.*

It is logical to follow someone that is making it happen. If you want something bad enough you will be willing to pay the price. You determine the goal you want to reach. The reward you will receive is built into that goal. The price is built in as well because the price you will pay is in direct relation to the reward.

In life, and in business, it is smart to look to others who have already achieved what you want to achieve. If you want to be a great parent, gather information from the greatest parent you know. Develop their habits. Habits control you—the way you think, eat, and work. You are a product of your habits—good or bad.

CSC: *"If I were just starting out in this business, what kind of people would you counsel me to look for?"*

DY: You have to decide what kind of business you want to run. If your goal is to have a successful, profitable, long-term business, then you want the kind of people who will accommodate that goal. Let's say you already own a major corporation. Would you bring in welfare mentality people to run that corporation? No! I think you would agree that you would handpick the sharpest, smartest, most motivated people you could find. This business is no different in that respect. If you prospect people who are lacking in ambition, motivation, desire, or integrity, you won't go very far.

Is our economy strong today because of the policies in Washington? NO! I say that business has made this economy. The thing that bothers me the most is that some people tear down the rich, saying that they are greedy and materialistic. I say that it is the individual that chooses his or her limits. My God says that life is unlimited! My goals and dreams are what set the bar for my work. Until I give my maximum, I won't reach my potential. When I give my maximum, whether in business or at the gym, I feel better about myself.

I believe that success is my right and my obligation. I think it is important to empower others with a dream. By doing so, you give others a vision and show people what is available to them if they are willing to work for it. We each have the responsibility to do the best we can. If you are a parent, your kids need you to set the example for them to follow. You should be their hero. How can you get your kids to set their standards high if you don't?

I am just a hard-working person with great faith! Birdie and I have forgotten more obstacles than most people have ever had. We just don't let circumstances stop us from our dreams. Imagine if you were a carpenter or a mechanic. Do you think you would get upset over a broken fingernail or busted knuckles? Do you think you would let that stop you from accomplishing your work or goal for the day? No!

CSC: *"Dexter, some people say that luck is involved in success. What do you say about that?"*

DY: At the gym, where I exercise and weight-train, I sometimes hear people say, "So and so is so lucky. She can eat anything she wants and look how great a figure she has." I say no, she works very hard to keep a great figure and a strong, healthy body. Those other people may have seen her eating an ice cream or whatever, but what they don't see is the hours of work, sweat, and energy she devotes at the gym in order to maintain that great shape and healthy body. We always have a choice in what we are going to reap. Success, like one's health, doesn't just happen. We reap what we sow.

CSC: *"On your road to success, you must have had some hurdles to overcome. Dex, what were the toughest obstacles you faced?"*

DY: I have had lots of obstacles, but the biggest one was the fact that I stuttered. In fact, I stuttered so badly I would miss school rather than have to stand up in front of anyone and speak out loud. I would rather fail the class than embarrass myself. Then I get involved in a business where my success is predicated on my ability to talk to other people—lots of them. If I could face my fears and my embarrassment, I knew I could make my dreams come true and give my wife and kids the life they deserved. So I started. I stuttered so badly, it took me four hours to give a two-hour presentation. I think I sponsored so many people in the beginning because when people sat through one of my business presentations they had to think, "If Dexter can do this, I certainly can!"

The second biggest hurdle was Birdie. It was hard on Birdie to let me go out and work the many hours it took in the beginning. We grew up in a mill town. Most of the people we knew worked at the mill or other blue-collar jobs. She was used to nine-to-five jobs where the husband pulled in the driveway by 5:30 every night. With our business I was on the road almost every night and often pulled in many hours after she had gotten the kids to bed and fallen asleep waiting on me. It was hard on Birdie.

The other part of the business that was tough on her was that instead of bringing home a pay check at the end of the week, I brought home a bonus check or commissions from product sales, most of which went directly back into our business. Birdie was 27 and taking care of seven little kids. We were broke. Even after I started making some money, I believed that we should wait, go without, until we could pay cash for what we wanted. Most of our friends lived on borrowed money. It is no different today. People live beyond their income and use credit cards and loans to support their whims of desire. Then they pay and they pay and they pay. I figured out that if I bought a nice used car and financed it for 24 months, paid it off early and kept it for four years, I could save the payment for the last two plus years, and after four years, I had enough money to pay cash for my next used car. I banked the money for another four years and then had enough money to buy a new one—in cash! People don't seem to understand that saving 20 percent a year is like earning 20 percent more income, tax-free! You just gave yourself a 20-percent raise. J.Paul Getty said, "It's not how much you make but how much you keep that counts."

It was hard on Birdie to do without for so many years, but she has lived a fabulous life for many, many years, and she will for the rest of her life. And as far as letting me go without her, we go everywhere together now. She's my sweetheart, my girlfriend, and my best friend. And all those people back in the little mill town, well, they were wrong about me.

CSC: *"Tell me more about what it was that made you push through your challenges, criticism, and fears?"*

DY: More than anything else it was my dream. You'll hear me say that a lot, but without a dream, nothing happens. Of course, you have to have faith and a good attitude, but without a dream, there is nothing, no gas in the tank so to speak. I had to have a vehicle to reach my dreams. That vehicle was Amway. I had to have a cause, a reason that was bigger than my fears. My biggest cause is Birdie. She is my queen and more than any other dream I have, I want to give her the lifestyle she deserves.

A man's personal ego needs to supply that lifestyle for his wife. I hear a lot of guys say that they want love from their wife, much more than they want a clean house. I say give them the lifestyle they want and deserve.

CSC: *"Dexter, why do you think Amway gets so much criticism?"*

DY: When your head is above the crowd you always get the most tomatoes. Our competition likes to criticize us because we are the best. When you talk to people about Amway, they either love it or hate it. Why? When you ask someone to join you in business and they don't do it, many of them have to have an excuse, a reason to justify why you are doing something different, making something work in your life and they are not. So they often criticize. What else can they do? They can't say, "I'm lazy." Or "I'm afraid of failing." So instead they say, "Your program stinks."

People who fight for strong ideals often find battles to overcome. We have a strong work ethic. We work to support the foundation of the family. If you stand for nothing, you'll fall for anything. The stronger you are, the more hits you'll take.

People who don't want to stand for something will find a way to justify their decision. They usually find fault with anyone or anything who is different, who stands for things they won't. Another thing people often do is to make a decision about our business based on the experience of someone they knew, or perhaps their own one-time attempt. They failed once and they are not trying again.

Before I met Birdie, I went steady with lots of girls. Why did I go out with so many? I was looking for the right one. Some of those girls were disappointing, some hurt me, some were wrong for me. But I had to go through them to find the right one. Had I not gone through all of them, I probably wouldn't have found Birdie. If you aren't willing to go through it, to do the searching, you won't get the prize! If I judged all girls on the first 10 or even 50, would I have found Birdie? I was willing to take some tomatoes.

Our company is the only network marketing company I know of where the second generation is taking over the business. Today, the DeVos and VanAndel children are starting a new company and reorganizing an old one. They are working with the field. We are the biggest company out there. We have the strongest financial backing. We have the best field leadership with long-term results. It's the leaders in the field who know the needs to keep moving forward. We have an independent elected board, the most progressive team that exists anywhere in the world. There is simply nothing like it in the industry.

CSC: *"People say that Quixtar is just Amway in a different set of clothes. Is that true? Tell me about Quixtar."*

DY: Amway was the first company that stuck, the first company that had tremendous success and growth. They have the strongest, the longest, and best track record, and are the most successful.

Many other MLM [multilevel marketing] companies have tried to duplicate their success. So, isn't any other MLM just a knock off of Amway? But are they? For example, the National Football League is just High School football at the next level. Quixtar is for the new generation. It is just a higher level. Quixtar is the future!

CSC: *"Where do you see the business in the next 30 years?"*

DY: Thirty years? I hope I'm here to see it. I think it will be bigger than any of us can imagine. The lifestyle I live today I couldn't even have dreamed of 10 years ago. When I was 25 I couldn't picture being 50. But I've been in Amway for 35 years. I have been married for 42 years. I am 60 years old today. But even at 50, I could not have predicted my life today. My dream wasn't that big. My biggest guys, my biggest leaders in the business, live better today than I did when I was at their level.

CSC: *"Dexter, I have heard that you have the largest organization in the world. What kind of lifestyle does that size of business give you?"*

DY: My business is worldwide. I have business in every market that is open in the world. My downline is larger than the entire downline of any company in network marketing. My track record is very good—35 years and building bigger everyday. Last year my income from this compensation plan alone was $5 million.

I got in the business to make $1,000 a month. I have seven kids who developed great habits based on the teaching of their parents. They each live better today than we did at their age.

Birdie and I bought a beautiful home on 14 acres on the waterway that runs out to the ocean on the west coast of Florida. Huge yachts go by all daylong. From the deck of our

12,000-square-foot home, we watch as huge yachts gracefully float down the waterway in front of our home. We have two 60-foot marinas and two other homes on our property. Our Florida home is so different from our log cabin in North Carolina. The master suite of our Florida home is 3,000 square feet. We have five kitchens and I forget how many baths! The entire home is modern décor and white carpet. When we moved down here, we took some of our personal clothes and items and hired an interior decorator to help us with the rest. Birdie and I chose hand-painted silk drapes and wallpaper.

We did bring some of our cars, boats, and personal belongings, but everything else is new. The closets in our home are the size of our old master bedroom. Our covered pool overlooks the waterway. Our homes are behind electric gates, and there is enough storage for my 30 automobiles. I like cars. Many of my cars are antiques. Birdie has a Mercedes convertible in Charlotte and another one in Florida. She has a Jaguar sedan in Charlotte and another one in Florida. We have a Cadillac El Dorado convertible, two Rolls Royce convertibles, two Rolls Royce sedans, one Mercedes sedan, many antique cars, and even a few Harleys.

Birdie and I fly around the world in one of our two private jets, and we enjoy the freedom our lifestyle gives us. When I am in Florida, I have a personal trainer five days a week and both Birdie and I have two-hour massages twice a week, whether traveling or at home.

CSC: *"Tell me about your other home in North Carolina."*

DY: In North Carolina our 16,000-square-foot log cabin is nestled in the trees just at the edge of a lake on 25 acres. We have a five-car garage on both ends of the cabin and a 14,000-square-foot guesthouse. When we land in North Carolina our stretch Lincoln limousine meets us with one of our two drivers in a police uniform. We always have police around for security. With a high level of security we always feel safe.

We enjoy eating out frequently with our best friends, our distributors. We stay out on the road until we are tired of it, then we head home until we get tired of that. It's great to have the freedom to make choices in your life. Anything Birdie wants, Birdie gets. She shops at elite boutiques and travels to exotic resorts. Her kids are her best friends. Three of them are business partners in several of our businesses. My brother is my partner in Yager Construction. We believe in living beneath our income. We invest. Our lifestyle is the product of good habits.

I am just another guy, a guy that decided to do something with his life. Everyone is important, they just need to learn to be important to themselves. Most people never empower themselves because they don't believe they deserve to succeed. If we would only live as big as others see us.

CSC: *"Dexter, you seem to have such a close relationship with Birdie. After 42 years of marriage, what is your secret?"*

DY: I have a very healthy, prosperous marriage. We live in our marriage in constant submission to each other. I am the leader of my family. I make all the major decisions, but all those decisions were to make a great lifestyle for Birdie. Sometimes I wonder who really is the boss? I say Birdie is!

Birdie bought me when I had no value. I was just a nice guy, respectful. She bet her whole life on me! I had a responsibility and obligation to take care of her. When I had a stroke the doctor's told me I'd never walk again. I offered Birdie a divorce. She had made a bad investment—me! It wasn't her fault that she got stuck with a guy that didn't take good care of his health. I didn't want to stick her with my deal. After I offered her a divorce, I laid in that bed and cried. She left a note on the pillow and told me that she loved me, that she wanted me, and that she believed in me. That girl was willing to bet on me again!

The Lord, my faith, and my wife are the most precious assets! The most important thing in my life is my best buddy, Birdie, who is on my arm next to me!

CSC: *"If you could offer one piece of advice to would-be successful entrepreneurs, what would it be?"*

DY: Get a big dream. Hold on to it. Keep it in front of you every day. You have to build depth and get your new people started by doing right things, creating right habits. Learn how to give people a reason to stay in! I never found people that wanted it as bad as me for as long as I have. Be a leader—leaders set the pace!

Index